The
big book
of conflict
resolution
games

Quick, Effective Activities to Improve Communication,
Trust, and Collaboration

Mary Scannell

New York Chicago San Francisco Lisbon London Madrid Mexico City
Milan New Delhi San Juan Seoul Singapore Sydney Toronto

Copyright © 2010 by The McGraw-Hill Companies, Inc. All rights reserved. Printed in the United States of America. Except as permitted under the United States Copyright Act of 1976, no part of this publication may be reproduced or distributed in any form or by any means, or stored in a database or retrieval system, without the prior written permission of the publisher.

1 2 3 4 5 6 7 8 9 10 11 12 13 14 15   WFR/WFR   1 9 8 7 6 5 4 3 2 1 0

ISBN   978-0-07-183671-5
MHID   0-07-174224-7

Library of Congress Cataloging-in-Publication Data

Scannell, Mary, 1959–
     The big book of conflict-resolution games : quick, effective activities to improve
     communication, trust, and collaboration / Mary Scannell.
            p.   cm.

     1. Conflict management.   2. Group games.   3. Management games.
     I. Title.

     HD42.S27   2010
     658.4′053—dc22   2010014894

Interior design by Think Book Works
Illustrations by Drake Carr and Jaclyn LaBarbera

McGraw-Hill books are available at special quantity discounts to use as premiums and sales promotions or for use in corporate training programs. To contact a representative, please e-mail us at bulksales@mcgraw-hill.com.

Contents

5   Perspective   159

6   EQ (Emotional Intelligence)   179

7 Collaboration 205

Acknowledgments

Ten years into my career as a corporate trainer, I "discovered" the world of experiential education. Suddenly, a new and more effective method of facilitation was opened up to me. For that, I am indebted to John Dewey, the "Father of Experiential Education," and to Karl Rohnke, who created the framework on which many of today's experiential activities are built.

My sincere gratitude to all of my corporate clients for granting me the privilege of working with their teams. And to those teams, thank you for your participation and your trust. I consider myself fortunate to be able to work with you and gain insight into your processes.

To Emily Carleton, my editor at McGraw-Hill, thank you for a great idea and for your confidence in my ability to make it work. My appreciation to Rena Copperman and her team for their dedication to this project and their attention to detail throughout the editing process. Thanks to Julia Anderson Bauer at McGraw-Hill for her guidance in the final stages of review and production. To Drake Carr, thank you for illustrations that add the perfect energy to the games. A special thanks to Jaclyn LaBarbera for dropping everything to provide some last-minute drawings.

My deepest gratitude to Karen, Mike, and Cathie for teaching me the skills necessary to resolve enormous conflict, as only siblings can do. For being there with support and encouragement whenever I need it, thank you to my dear friends Cindy, Sandi, and Michelle.

Thank you to my mom, Alice, my dad, Ed, and the rest of my family, for your love and laughter.

And most of all to my husband, Kerry, I couldn't have done it without you.

Introduction

In the middle of difficulty lies opportunity.

—*Albert Einstein*

Conflict in the workplace is: (a) avoidable, (b) preventable, (c) necessary, or **(d) all of the above**.

Conflict is a natural and normal feature of the workplace. It occurs in every organization. For any team that strives to attain its goals, conflict is inevitable. Although differences will occur, the outcome doesn't have to be negative. Conflict can provide opportunities. Conflict challenges us to think harder, to be more creative, to develop greater understanding, and to search for alternative avenues that are more efficient, more effective, and more productive.

Unresolved conflict, however, can result in the breakdown of a group. When unaddressed conflict occurs in the workplace, it can reduce morale, hamper performance, and increase absenteeism. It leads to increased stress among employees, decreased productivity, and at worst, aggression or violence. Studies show that managers spend at least 25 percent of their time resolving workplace conflicts. This affects the output of the work group and can have a profound impact on organizational performance.

Conflict, like any other key business process, must be managed. The conflict resolution games in this book are designed to allow team members to increase their ability to resolve conflict and ultimately transform conflict into collaboration.

Games and activities create a safe environment for team members to experience real conflict—complete with emotions, assumptions, and communication challenges. Because games often mimic the characteristics of real-life situations, especially in the realms of competition and cooperation, games can reveal the typical way conflict is dealt with in the team. Teams can begin to understand their usual reactions, and then go on to discover more effective strategies for dealing with similar situations.

Experiential activities allow team members to practice their reactions to conflict and their subsequent actions. Consequently, in future workplace conflicts, they will have the tools and the experience to bring about positive results. By participating in conflict-resolution games, team members build trust, improve communication, and challenge ineffective processes to create a team that is more productive and more effective.

Components of Conflict

Conflict arises from a clash of perceptions, goals, or values in a domain where people care about the outcome. The seeds of conflict may be sown in confusion about, or disagreement with, the common purpose and how to achieve it. Further, pursuing common goals may interfere with achieving individual goals within the organization.

When it comes to conflict, various differences may be involved. Team members may differ on what the problem is; or, they may agree on what the problem is but have a different perspective about it; or, they may share the same perspective but have different ideas on how to solve the problem.

- **Communication**—Communication can both cause and remedy conflict. As with other workplace skills, effective communication must be learned. A lack of open communication tends to drive conflict underground, and can create a downward spiral of misunderstanding and hostility. Effective communication (including active listening) is the means by which disagreement can be prevented, managed, or resolved.
- **Competition**—The competition for limited resources will certainly generate conflict. Time, money, space, materials, supplies, and equipment are all valuable commodities. Competition for any of these resources will inevitably lead to interpersonal or interdepartmental conflict. Whenever workers compete for scarce resources, recognition, or position in the organization's hierarchy, conflict can occur.

- **Inconsistency**—Whenever company policies are changed, inconsistently applied, or nonexistent, misunderstandings are likely to occur. Associates need to know and understand company rules and policies; they should not have to guess. Inconsistency in the workplace is a common source of conflict.
- **Diversity**—Individuals are individuals, and they differ in many ways. These differences are often a starting point for conflict. There are various styles for the way we deal with people and problems. Team members need to understand their own style and learn how to accept differing styles. Conflict can also be caused by differing personal values. "Factions" in the workplace can lead to gossip, suspicion, and ultimately conflict. The group must learn to accept diversity in the workplace and to work as a team. Emphasizing differences helps team members look for common ground.

    Most teams are diverse in age, gender, culture, experience, and knowledge. They may also be diverse in race, creed, religion, or disability. While all this diversity may result in conflict, teams that learn to embrace their differences and value new ideas can turn conflict into creative collaboration.
- **Perspective**—Just as two or more workers can have conflicting styles, they can also have conflicting perceptions. They may view the same incident in dramatically different ways. For example, we now have four generations in the workplace. Each generation brings a different perspective.
- **Interdependency**—Interdependency and increased interaction within an organization are also sources of conflict. The more often people interact, the more potential there is for conflict. Conflicting pressures can occur when two or more associates or departments are responsible for separate actions with the same deadline. Interdependency requires that people understand others' points of view, needs, and priorities. Teamwork and increasing levels of participation within an organization will require a greater need for conflict resolution skills.
- **Emotional Intelligence**—Emotional intelligence is a personal attribute that is very useful in reducing conflict. The amount of an individual's emotional intelligence is referred to as that person's emotional

intelligence quotient, or EQ. People with high EQs are empathetic and sensitive to the feelings of others. Dealing with associates as human beings with real lives is often overlooked in the busy workplace. People with high emotional intelligence can do this in a professional manner, while maintaining appropriate boundaries. The good news is that anyone can raise his or her EQ by developing the skills to effectively combine professionalism with emotions like sensitivity and empathy.

The Costs of Ignoring Conflict

Often, people fear conflict and see it as something to avoid. Some may even have the impression that all conflict is bad. Because conflict is a subject where there is a tendency to feel great discomfort, many may choose to simply ignore conflict. The danger in this approach is that the conflict festers under the surface and then bubbles up in subtle ways. Perhaps a team member is unresponsive to an e-mail request; or someone refuses to ask for help and consequently takes far longer than necessary on a task; or people simply avoid each other. Conflict under the surface is very disruptive. It fractures a team as people choose sides and try to build up their forces. It fosters competition, distrust, poor communication, and low productivity.

While conflict may be easy to avoid or ignore in the short term, this will result in unresolved conflict costs. These costs can include turnover, increased absenteeism, health problems, and even stress-related workers' compensation claims. The use of valuable resources to address and resolve conflict early, and to improve communication in the workplace, is a necessary part of doing business.

Transforming Conflict into Collaboration

Engaging in conflict doesn't have to be negative or counterproductive. In fact, it can be positive. Conflict can be helpful in making necessary changes within a work environment. When faced with conflict, there are five different strategies to deal with the situation:

- **Ignore**—We could put off doing anything at all.
- **Win-Lose**—We may choose to exert control and "win" over our opponent.
- **Lose-Win**—We may choose to acquiesce and "give in" to the other person.
- **Lose-Lose**—We could agree on a compromise, where both parties give something up.
- **Win-Win**—We could choose an option where those involved in the conflict work together to discover a *win-win* solution—a collaborative solution.

Anyone who takes the time to study conflict understands its power to transform what exists into something better. That does not make conflict easy, but it does make it easier to accept as a natural part of our lives. Once we make this mental switch, we can even begin to embrace the idea of conflict and the lessons that come with it. A thoughtful response to conflict strengthens the team and sets the stage to resolve the conflict. We get a chance to know our team better, to build trust, and to create clearer communication.

Because our typical knee-jerk reaction to conflict is to fight back or compete, a collaborative approach is often counterintuitive. Games reveal to teams their reactions to conflict, demonstrate the consequences of those reactions, and then point the way to better strategies—all while the participants are having fun.

Conflict can clear the underlying tensions and bring out issues so the team can deal with them and learn from them. However, just because conflict can produce a beneficial outcome does not mean it's comfortable. Still, the best approach is for a team to deal with conflict and to accept that it's a normal part of working together, and that it can even benefit the group. Conflict—in the right setting, handled in the right way—can be constructive. It is through conflict that an awareness of the need for some necessary changes can be found.

Why Use Conflict-Resolution Games?

Games can reveal real conflict—along with emotions, personalities, misunderstandings, and reactions. Through games, the team experiences conflict in a safe environment. Competent facilitation is the key. As facilitator, you need to be aware of what's going on, take notes, encourage, redirect, and even stop activities for a mid-activity discussion if necessary. Engaging in conflict can be delicate territory for many on the team, so you need to provide support and encouragement as they practice the skills and get comfortable using them.

You will notice many of these games recommend small teams—this is to keep all participants involved in the process. Another way to maximize participation is to use "observers" who can provide excellent "big picture" feedback during the debriefing discussion. To maintain a high level of participation throughout the game and during the debriefing process, consider passing out the discussion questions found at the end of the games to small teams for a self-debriefing prior to the large group discussion. This will ensure that everyone relates the experience to their situation and contributes to the discussion. Just as important as getting everyone involved in the game is getting everyone involved in the discussion, where the bulk of the learning takes place.

When teams learn the benefits of conflict, they begin to lose some of the fear associated with conflict. Team-building games are the perfect way for a team to experience such benefits. The debriefing discussion for many of the conflict-resolution games takes longer than the actual activity, because attendees are changing some core behaviors and beliefs regarding conflict. Make sure you allot plenty of time for the discussion, because cutting it short denies the team the necessary time it takes for some to make the shift.

The games in this book will help the team become aware of and practice the characteristics and skills necessary to resolve—or transform—conflict. You will find games that build trust, improve EQ, enhance verbal and nonverbal communication, challenge assumptions, and appreciate diversity. Use these games to empower your teams to search for collaborative solutions in conflict situations. Use these games to allow teams to experience the result of effectively transforming conflict into collaboration. Use these games to take your team from a group of individuals to a high-performing team.

Facilitation

The role of the facilitator is critical to a team's successful navigation through the conflict process. The facilitator needs to pay close attention to team members as they experience the process. The actions of the team can provide insight for the debrief discussion. The facilitator also benefits from a high EQ, which allows him or her to notice the underlying emotions the team may be experiencing. During the debriefing discussion at the end of each activity, it's important for the facilitator to ensure everyone's involvement. This maintains a high level of engagement as team members transfer the game to real life and helps to build confidence in the new skills.

Conflict is healthy for a team as long as it is handled in an effective manner. By engaging in conflict-resolution activities, participants may become more accepting of others' beliefs, perspectives, and experiences. Interacting on the informal level that conflict-resolution games provide can change attitudes and behavior, ultimately providing an opportunity to build a more cohesive and trusting team. Some may be hesitant to participate because of the subject matter, but with appropriate climate-setting and rapport-building activities, and competent facilitation, they can ease into the games naturally. You may well discover that the more resistant the participant, the more dramatic the result.

Once team members have experienced the benefits of dealing with conflict—saving time, increased trust, stronger relationships, enhanced creativity, and more open communication—they are usually more likely to embrace conflict than deny it. Even though they may feel ready to embrace conflict, it can still be daunting; after all, it may be completely new territory for some. It is essential for the facilitator to allow team members to practice real conflict in order to experience the actual process, which is the same in games and in life. A team that feels empowered to do this becomes a resilient, powerful, and effective team. The group will transform into a team that looks for the answers within—a team with individuals who trust and respect one another.

Leadership

If management wants the team to realize the full potential of conflict-resolution games, they must get involved in the process. Conflict resolution is an ongoing process for every team, and it's important that leadership understands the skills necessary to build a team that is confident in their ability to experience conflict and to transform that conflict into something healthy and productive. When leaders are aware of the skills necessary to do this, they can reinforce and encourage the continued use of those skills. Those in leadership roles can provide a supportive environment by allowing time for regular team meetings, along with activities that keep these skills fresh, and by broadening the comfort zone for using the skills throughout the entire team.

Benefits of Conflict-Resolution Games

The topic of conflict fits perfectly with the idea of games. Games are inherently competitive. Competition breeds conflict. In competitive situations, there is generally a winner and a loser. In a compromise, a team may accept something lesser without considering other options. The ultimate goal of conflict games is to reveal collaborative solutions. Experiential learning activities and exercises can challenge a team to deal with the real issues of conflict—differing personality styles, perceptions, assumptions, and ways of thinking—and provide skills that can be used in real life.

The best feature of games is that they allow teams to practice new skills in a fun and engaging manner. When participants are engaged in the process, they take ownership of the techniques they learn, they remember the concepts, and they get comfortable using the skills. As they become more at ease with the concepts, it is more likely they will use the skills in the workplace. Here's why:

- Games help the team *experience the process*. They experience the conflict process in a fun, supportive environment that enables the team to create effective strategies and practice the skills necessary to resolve conflict.

- Games help the team *understand key points*—points that are relevant, clear, and memorable. Games are powerful tools to drive home key ideas.
- Games help *build morale.* They provide a context for team members to take control of their learning and create the energy to make it fun in the process.
- Games help team members learn to *trust each other.* They provide opportunities for sharing insights, emotions, and experiences as the team develops solutions. Increased understanding and appreciation for each other's viewpoints are valuable by-products of the discussion during the activity debriefing.
- Games help team members *become more flexible and adaptive.* Members soon understand and appreciate the fact that there may be more than one way to solve a problem.
- Games provide opportunities for team leaders to *reinforce appropriate behaviors.* When cooperation is displayed, when active listening is demonstrated, or when trust is extended, a leader can show appreciation for the desirable responses elicited from a team-building game and debriefing session.
- Games *provide opportunities to connect.* When we feel connected, we are more likely to look for a way to collaborate rather than compete.

Characteristics of Conflict-Resolution Games

The games in this book are appropriate to use in training sessions and team meetings, as well as team-building programs. You may also want to try them as activities during open discussions or grievance airings. These games include the following features:

1. They are *impactful.* While the games themselves take little time (some as little as 15 minutes), the lessons learned leave a lasting impression.

2. They are *inexpensive.* There are very few props necessary, and many of the props can be reused again and again before needing replacement.
3. They are *participative.* The games involve the entire team—no one sits on the sidelines. Games help participants focus their energy and attention, therefore making them think, interact, and have fun—all while learning to be better team players.
4. They are *engaging.* Because team members find solutions to the challenges collaboratively, they are engaged throughout the process.

These games will prove to be effective time and time again.

Your Keys to Success

Act as if what you do makes a difference. It does.

—*William James*

Embrace the Idea That Conflict Can Be Positive

Teams can get complacent and comfortable. Comfort and complacency are often the enemies of creativity and energy. Conflict can be a great catalyst for creative energy. Groups that learn to navigate through conflict and use it to their benefit can become highly motivated and effective teams.

For the team to buy into the idea that conflict can be a good thing, the facilitator needs to believe it. There are many excellent books and Web sites that the facilitator can look to for information. Armed with the evidence, it's easy to get excited about the idea of helping participants make this realization for themselves. Take a look at all the activities in this book before deciding which will be the best games for your team at this particular time.

Invest the Time

Facilitating an experiential session on conflict resolution can take some time. Before committing to the topic, make sure you have ample time to allow the team to have the experience and also enough time for an insightful and meaningful debriefing discussion. If time is short, consider an activity that builds trust or improves communication or even an activity that fosters a sense of community within the team. These activities are excellent predecessors to a conflict-resolution games session.

Allow the Games to Work

All of these conflict-resolution games work. They are tried, tested, and proven. The power of games is that no two processes will be exactly alike. Trust that although a game may progress differently than anticipated, it will ultimately provide the lesson that the team needs. This process can be hindered by a facilitator who tries to take too much control. Relax and let the game unfold as it will.

Anticipate Resistance

You may see initial hesitation from some participants because of the topic or the experiential nature of the approach. Do your best to accept this natural response and you might even mention it in your introduction. When it comes to experiential learning, it's best to let participants know at the beginning of a session that some games may not be a good "fit" for each participant, but there are other ways they can contribute to the team during an activity. They can serve as observers, providing valuable insight and a different perspective during the group discussion. You can provide observers with an observation tracking sheet to keep everyone engaged throughout the process.

Allow the Team to Work Through Frustration

Frustration is to be expected in some of these activities. Frustration can lead to conflict, which can lead a team to discover effective strategies to handle conflict. Sometimes that requires a facilitator to hold his or her tongue and allow the group the opportunity to experience the natural process of conflict resolution. Always use common sense, as there will be times that a mid-activity discussion will enhance the experience and maintain the high participation level of all team members.

One of the most useful things a facilitator can do to enrich the debriefing discussion is to take notes throughout the activity. If your groups are large, you may find it more effective to let them debrief in smaller teams, which will encourage more participation. The facilitator does not have to be a part of every debriefing discussion to make it meaningful to the participants. Be prepared with copies of the discussion questions to distribute to the teams so they can lead their own debriefing discussion.

Use Common Sense

There is some movement required in some of the games. Invite your participants to use their common sense. If an activity is not a good physical fit for a team member, there are always other contributions he or she can make to maintain a high level of involvement. Many of these games benefit from one or more observers, which is a less physical role.

Do Your Homework

Facilitating a program on conflict resolution is not for the novice trainer. It is a good idea to get some experience, and get comfortable with the process of experiential training, before tackling the challenge of facilitating a team through conflict. More so than other topics, conflict tends to take team members outside their comfort zones, and without proper lead-in activities, they may even be pushed to their panic zones. If this occurs, you may find that some participants will shut down, doing themselves and the team no good at all. Of course, even with ample lead-in and comfort-building activities, this may occur—be ready for it and use it in the debriefing discussion. Be there to provide encouragement and support throughout the game.

Is Conflict Really a Game?

Games fit the topic of conflict resolution very well. Many games have an element of innate or assumed competition. When we compete, we position ourselves against one another, which leads to conflict. That conflict exists is a given; whether the team is comfortable enough to experience the conflict process is another matter. Conflict that is allowed to linger beneath the surface can be very detrimental to a team. Team members may guard information, distrust one another, and form alliances. As a result, productivity plummets. Games allow the team to experience the process; transform conflict into collaboration; and practice the skills in a fun, informal, and effective manner.

Stay on Track During the Debriefing Discussion

Because some of these games reveal buried emotions, the debriefing discussions can easily go off on tangents or become gripe sessions, which can be unproductive. Be prepared to redirect the group discussion if this happens. Invite team members to come to you during breaks or at the conclusion of the session for a continuation of the discussion.

Be Flexible

During some games—for example, Helium Hoop—you may notice that frustrations are running so high that communication is completely breaking down and team members are blaming and verbally attacking one another. Be prepared to cut the activity, lead a debriefing discussion, go on to other activities, and eventually come back to it later, after learning some helpful skills in conflict resolution.

Practice, Practice, Practice

Most games books recommend that facilitators practice the activities before "taking them live." Let's all admit that there have been times when we have ignored that advice. When the topic is conflict, it is definitely not the time to ignore that advice. Practice these games with your family, friends, or colleagues so that you can be comfortable enough with the game to focus your attention on what is going on with the team. That way, when you do "take it live," you are 100 percent there for the team, taking notes and observing the nuances of the activity. You will also be able to anticipate where the team may go and be ready to let that unfold without being wrapped up in the technicalities of the game.

Dust Off Some "Classics"

You may see a couple of games in this book that are already familiar. Before skipping over these classics, take a quick look at how these standards have been adapted to help facilitate the concept of conflict resolution. The benefit of choosing a classic is that you may already have a level of comfort facilitating the game, and attendees may have a level of familiarity with the game. It is the conflict resolution twists that make the activity impactful and meaningful. An example is the game Two Truths and a Lie—With a Twist! Many of us have played Two Truths and a Lie, but with the twist, this game can be a very powerful lesson in how prejudging affects relationships within a team.

Have Fun Out There

Games are fun. Even with a serious topic, allow the group (and yourself) to have some fun with it. They will stay engaged and participate more fully, and, as a result, the lessons will stay with them longer. You will establish a better comfort zone, which will lead to greater trust in you and will allow you to take the team further.

How to Use This Book

Conflict-Resolution Games

Like that old cliché about love and hate, there is often a thin line between conflict and collaboration. With the skills and tools outlined in this book, conflict can often be transformed into collaboration. The games in this book are a special set of activities and exercises designed to: (1) understand conflict, (2) improve communication, (3) value diversity, (4) build trust, (5) provide perspective, (6) raise EQ (emotional intelligence), and (7) foster collaboration.

Many of these games provide a valuable lesson whether or not the participants succeed in a task. This is because the focus is on the process, the debriefing discussion, and how the experience can be applied to the workplace. As an added bonus, games allow team members to have fun while learning.

Selecting an Appropriate Conflict-Resolution Game

As you look through this book, you'll notice that each conflict-resolution game has a distinct purpose, a recommended group size, a list of materials needed, and an estimated time requirement. Let these guidelines help you determine the appropriate games for your groups or meetings.

It's a good idea to begin with activities that support conflict resolution, such as communication activities or trust-building activities. As participants get comfortable with each other and begin to understand the skills necessary to resolve conflict, you can then choose activities that are more challenging. Here is a brief overview of the seven chapters in this book:

1. **Conflict**—Conflict is a natural occurrence in any group or team. The games found in this chapter will allow team members to experience real conflict, work together to find real solutions, and discover the tools that will allow them to transform future conflicts.

2. **Communication**—Effective communication skills, specifically listening and engaging in true dialogue, can transform conflict. The goal is to turn the conflict into a discussion, which requires us to overcome emotions, engage our brain, and use active listening skills. The games in this chapter provide insight into the importance of communication and present opportunities to practice effective communication skills.

3. **Diversity**—A football team of 11 quarterbacks or 11 linebackers probably won't do very well. Diversity gives teams a distinct advantage. The more diverse the group is, the more effective the team can be. The games in this chapter help the team to discover and appreciate the diversity of the team.

4. **Trust**—Trust is the glue that holds a group together, especially when experiencing conflict. The trust activities in this chapter help a group to build a level of comfort with each other and to demonstrate reliability and credibility.

5. **Perspective**—The games in this chapter will expose our unique perspective and make us aware of others' perspectives, while providing opportunities to understand how those perspectives may limit our ability to resolve conflict.

6. **Emotional Intelligence**—Empathy and sensitivity can help team members interact more effectively. These EQ games will help to build a better awareness of ourselves, and of the others on our team.

7. **Collaboration**—The willingness to explore win-win solutions during conflict can be reframed as the inclination to collaborate. Those involved must treat one another with equal importance and respect. This sometimes requires changing deeply ingrained assumptions that influence how we understand the situation and then taking action. These games will give teams a chance to experience real conflict and work together to create a collaborative outcome.

Preparing Game Materials

You will find it helpful to keep a supply of basic props that are often used in these conflict resolution games. Index cards, markers, painter's tape, tennis balls, a deck of cards, rope, flip-chart paper, and assorted office supplies can all be useful. It is also worthwhile to look ahead and anticipate which games may be appropriate for a given group or meeting. After selecting one or more games, you can save time by preparing your handouts, flip charts, or presentations in advance.

Introducing a Game

In general, give a brief explanation and background for a game. It is important to provide a context for the activity to help the team see where it fits into the program's agenda. Get their attention, solicit their cooperation, and share appropriate information, such as any rules or guidelines. Remind participants to use their common sense and to take an appropriate role during the game, as either an active participant or an active observer. Then assign them their task, along with any time limits. Make sure to monitor the activity as it progresses, allowing ample time for the debriefing discussion.

Leading a Team Discussion

Games will remain just that, games, in the absence of an effective facilitated debriefing discussion. Look over the provided materials ahead of time. Anticipate probable results and reactions. Take notes throughout the activity. In addition to the discussion questions provided with the game's instructions, you may want to prepare other questions that are more tailored to suit your particular group or purpose. Indicate the time limits for the discussion. Focus the team's attention on the meaning and purpose behind the game. Encourage the participants to be responsible for generating meaningful conversation; don't be too quick to insert your own opinions and observations. Keep the discussion flowing, but also get comfortable with pauses as group members formulate their ideas and conclusions. End the discussion when all major points have been addressed.

About Debriefing

Debriefing is the key to the learning experience. Without it, participants may not see the connection between what happened during the game and what happens in "real life." They may not understand the relevance of their actions in the game until they discuss the debriefing questions. To help the discussion flow just as smoothly as the game flowed, follow these guidelines:

- Take notes during the activity for reference during the debriefing discussion.
- Provide observers with an observation sheet to focus their attention during the game.
- Provide individuals with a copy of the discussion questions so they can note what they experienced during the game, before the full group discussion.
- For large groups, have participants discuss the debriefing questions in small teams before the group discussion to ensure everyone gets a chance to contribute.
- Get participants to discuss what happened in the game, what they learned, and how the learning applies in the workplace.
- Ask open-ended questions for a meaningful discussion.
- Ask—don't tell—participants about their experience, and how it relates to real-life situations.
- Use the discussion questions provided with each game as guidelines, not as a manual to be followed exactly.
- Adapt the ideas to what really happened in each game and what is really happening in the workplace. All circumstances will differ.

Making the Transition to Applications

All of the games in this book are generic, meaning that they are broad in nature and not restricted to any single organization or industry. Your debriefing discussion, however, can be tailored to meet the specific needs of your group. As the facilitator, it is imperative that you shift the team's attention from what happened in the activity to what is significant about the results. Encourage participants to consider questions like, "What will we remember from the game tomorrow?" "What can we take from this experience?" and "How can we use this experience to improve our team's performance?" You may consider making a record of the key learning points raised and action plans developed to distribute to the group for later review and follow-up.

Summary

Conflict is a natural occurrence in any group. The games and activities presented in this book are designed to resolve conflict and ultimately transform the energy of conflict into collaboration. Games facilitate learning and development of trust to help improve team performance, while injecting some fun in the process.

1

Understanding Conflict

Don't fight forces, use them.

—R. Buckminster Fuller

How Do You See It?

Group Size

Any

Materials

One copy of the Conflict—How Do You See It? handout (provided) for each participant, pens

Time

30 to 40 minutes

Procedure

Conflict can provide the spark that often leads to better solutions, creativity, and collaboration. This activity helps team members to: (1) become more comfortable with conflict, (2) consider the positive aspects of conflict, and (3) understand the possible benefits to themselves and the team.

Have participants pair up. Provide each person with a copy of the handout. Allow 10 to 15 minutes for partners to interview each other. Follow with a group discussion of the interviews and then go over the discussion questions.

Tips

Follow this activity with the game Positive Spin.

Variations

Have team members switch partners every three questions to increase the level of trust within the team.

Discussion Questions

1. Were your partner's perspectives different from your perspective?

2. What were some things you learned by considering another's perspective?

3. Does discussing conflict like this make it "less scary"? In what ways?

4. Is conflict good or bad?

5. What are some ways in which conflict is detrimental to the team?

6. What are some ways in which conflict enriches the team?

Conflict—How Do You See It?

1. How do you define conflict?

_____

_____

2. What is your typical response to conflict?

_____

_____

3. What is your greatest strength when dealing with conflict?

_____

_____

4. If you could change one thing about the way you handle conflict, what would it be? Why?

_____

_____

5. What is the most important outcome of conflict?

_____

_____

6. In what ways have you seen your team benefit from conflict?

_____

_____

7. How can conflict be detrimental to a team?

_____

_____

8. What do you do when someone avoids conflict with you?

_____

_____

9. What are some reasons you choose to avoid conflict?

_____

_____

10. What can you do to promote a healthy attitude toward conflict within your team?

_____

_____

Positive Spin

OBJECTIVES
- To change our perspective on conflict in the workplace
- To consider the positive aspects of conflict

Group Size

Any

Materials

Flip-chart paper, markers, pens, one copy of the Team Debriefing Discussion Questions handout (provided) for each team

Time

20 to 40 minutes

Procedure

Split large groups into smaller teams of four to seven (having at least three teams is desirable). Have each team send a member up to collect their supplies, which consist of a sheet of flip-chart paper, some assorted markers, pens, and the handout.

Tell the teams that they are to write their definition of *conflict*. Their challenge is to define *conflict* without using negative terms. Once team members agree on a definition, have them write it on their flip-chart paper along with an illustration. Before the group presentations and discussion, have each team answer the debriefing questions on the handout.

After all teams are finished, have the teams present their ideas to the group. Hang up the flip-chart pages on the wall of the room for the duration of the training day.

Tips

Whenever possible, refer to the teams' definitions during the debriefing discussions.

Discussion Questions

1. How does the definition of conflict affect the way we think about conflict?

2. What are some negative consequences of conflict?

3. What are some positive outcomes of conflict?

4. List four potential positive outcomes of conflict in an organization.

Team Debriefing
Discussion Questions

1. How does the definition of *conflict* affect the way we think about conflict?

_____

_____

2. What are some negative consequences of conflict?

_____

_____

3. What are some positive outcomes of conflict?

_____

_____

4. List four potential positive outcomes of conflict in an organization.

- _____

- _____

- _____

- _____

Step by Step

Group Size

Any

Materials

Copy paper, markers, painter's tape

Time

15 to 20 minutes

Procedure

Split your group into smaller teams of four to seven participants. Station the teams in different areas throughout the room. Ask each team to write the word *Conflict* on one sheet of paper and the word *Resolution* on another. Instruct them to tape the sheets of paper about six feet apart on a nearby wall. Invite the teams to brainstorm the specific steps necessary to get from "Conflict" to "Resolution." As the steps are agreed upon, have team members write them on sheets of paper and place them on the wall between the "Conflict" and "Resolution" sheets.

Tips

- Use this activity as a part of a debriefing discussion early in your program after an activity such as Helium Hoop.
- Use these steps in the Quotable Quotes activity.

- If participants are having trouble, you may suggest that they reverse-engineer the steps.
- Have the team test the steps by using them in a conflict-resolution activity.

Discussion Questions

1. What has to happen right before "Resolution"?

2. Is there an additional step after "Resolution"? What could be added?

3. How does it benefit us to have a step-by-step approach to conflict?

4. How can we remember these steps in conflict situations?

Conflict Close-Up

Group Size

Any

Materials

None

Time

5 to 10 minutes

Procedure

Stand in the center of the room and announce the following to the group:

I am conflict. Consider how you typically react when you experience a personal conflict. Position yourself, in relation to me, somewhere in the room in a way that conveys your initial response to a conflict. Pay attention to your body language as well as your distance from the conflict.

Tips

Use this activity twice—once near the beginning of the program and then again at the end—to get a visual picture regarding changes in positions as a result of considering conflict differently.

Discussion Questions

1. What are some reasons you are standing where you are?

2. If where you are standing signifies your initial reaction, where might you stand after taking some time to think about the conflict?

3. What are some things that would cause you to move?

4. How might our reactions influence the course of the conflict?

Bull's-Eye

OBJECTIVES
- To understand that how we deal with conflict impacts ourselves, our team, and the organization
- To look at the big-picture benefits of effective conflict resolution

Group Size
Any
Materials
Flip-chart paper, markers, paper, pens
Time
15 to 20 minutes

Procedure

Draw a large target (consisting of three circles, one inside the other) on the flip-chart paper.

- The innermost circle represents the team members themselves.
- The middle circle represents the team.
- The outer circle represents the company.

Ask, "How does effectively resolving conflicts affect you, your team, and your organization?" As team members shout out various ideas, record them in the appropriate place on the target.

Tips

To allow participants time to contemplate the issue, have teams of four to seven draw individual targets and take a few minutes to fill in the circles on their own before the group discussion.

Variations

Create two targets: one for the benefits of effective conflict resolution and one for ineffective conflict management skills, and how each impacts the individual, the team, and the organization.

Discussion Questions

1. How does your ability to resolve conflicts affect you in your job?

2. How does a team member's ability to resolve conflicts impact the team?

3. How does a team's ability to resolve conflicts impact the organization?

Note to Self

Group Size
Any

Materials
Copies of Note to Self handout (provided), paper, pens, one envelope for each person

Time
10 to 20 minutes

Procedure
Ask participants to write a letter to themselves using the handout as a guideline. After the letters are completed, have each participant place his or her letter in an envelope and write his or her name on the envelope. Collect all the envelopes. At the conclusion of the program, give participants their envelopes and have them assess their progress by completing the "Post-Program" sentences.

Tips
With large groups, have small teams of four to seven debrief by discussing the post-training portion of the handout.

Discussion Questions

1. How were your expectations met today?

2. What are some things you need to work on?

3. What is your plan to improve those skills?

4. What were you surprised to discover?

Note to Self

Pre-Training

1. What do I need from this training?

_____

_____

2. What are some things I already know about this topic?

_____

_____

3. What do I expect to be able to do that I can't do now?

_____

_____

4. What do I need from the other members of my team?

_____

_____

5. What can I contribute to my team?

_____

_____

Post-Training

1. My expectations were met by . . .

_____

_____

2. I need to work on . . .

_____

_____

3. I was surprised to discover . . .

_____

_____

4. I commit to improving these skills . . .

_____

_____

Anything Goes

Group Size
Any
Materials
None
Time
10 to 20 minutes

Procedure

This game is a great way for participants to engage in a mini-conflict with another team member in a non-threatening manner. Ask participants to find a partner. Have each pair stand face to face, right fist out (as in Rock, Paper, Scissors), and say together, "Nothing, something, anything!" Once the word *anything* is said, the two participants yell out the name of any item they can think of (dog, coffee mug, shoe). After yelling out their items, team members must now debate one another as to why their item would "beat" the other person's item. Allow about two or three minutes of debate, then call a brief time-out to discuss the difference between debate and dialogue. After that, have the team continue with their conversations, only now, encourage team members to engage in dialogue—asking questions and listening to the answers—to come to an agreement between the two of them.

Tips

The essential difference between debate and dialogue is that true dialogue is collaborative. Participants are working toward shared understanding and strength and value in each other's positions. A debate is a discussion with the goal of persuading or advocating for their own view, attempting to prove the other side wrong, and searching for flaws and weaknesses in the other's positions. In dialogue, the intention is to really listen to one another's perspective with a willingness to be influenced by what we hear. Dialogue allows people to develop understanding for one another's perspectives, thoughts, and feelings as well as to reevaluate their own position in light of the other's understanding. In dialogue, everyone has a chance to be heard, understood, and to learn from each other.

Discussion Questions

1. How did you react to your mini-conflict?

2. Is this how you normally act in conflict situations? Why or why not?

3. How were you able to come to a consensus?

4. What happened when you switched from debate to dialogue?

5. When someone disagrees with you, do you always stop to ask questions?

6. Is it difficult to listen when someone disagrees with you? Why?

7. What made it easier in this activity?

8. In what ways could you use these skills the next time you're in conflict with another person?

Beach Ball Pass

Group Size

Any

Materials

Inflatable beach ball for each team

Time

15 to 20 minutes

Procedure

Break any large groups into smaller teams of eight to 15. The team begins by standing in a circle. The facilitator hits the ball into the circle and tells the team that they need to hit the ball twice as many times as there are team members (eight members need 16 hits). The only rules are that no team member can hit the ball twice in a row, or volley the ball back and forth over and over with another member.

Because this game is more difficult than it first appears, conflict may erupt early on as the team realizes this and has to regroup and devise a plan. Once the team achieves their goal number of hits, give them the next challenge, which is to hit the ball an equal number of times as there are team members. This time there is a new rule: each team member can hit the ball only one time. Even though this is a more difficult version, they should be able to build on what they have already learned to achieve success without conflict.

Tips

This activity requires some space and is best played outdoors (which can make it even more difficult due to weather conditions such as wind).

Discussion Questions

1. Was this activity more difficult than you originally thought it would be?
2. If so, did your assumptions lead to any communication challenges or conflict?
3. How did you and your team deal with the conflict?
4. In the second round, the goal was even more difficult. Did you experience the same communication or conflict challenges as the first round? Why or why not?
5. In what ways can you apply what you discovered in this game to the workplace?

Helium Hoop

Group Size

Any

Materials

Lightweight hula hoop for each team (not the kind filled with water)

Time

30 minutes

Procedure

This classic activity is unparalleled in its ability to induce conflict in a team. Break a large group into smaller teams of about seven (which is usually the maximum you can get around a hula hoop). Each team gets a hoop. Demonstrate the hand-holding technique they are required to use during the activity. Have team members bend their elbows with their hands out in front of them, palms facing in. Then have them close their hands so they are pointing at the person across the hoop from them. This hand position needs to be maintained for the duration of the activity. This prevents them from grasping the hoop. Place the hoop on top of the team's pointer-fingers to begin.

The goal of the activity is to simply lower the hoop to the ground. Every team member's fingers must maintain contact with the hoop at all times. If anyone loses contact or his or her fingers slip off the hoop, the team must assume the starting position and begin again.

Once the team understands the team goal and the rules, place the hoop in the starting position and begin. Usually the hoop starts to rise, as if by magic (I have even had participants ask me where I get the hoops filled with helium). Conflict ensues as team members, convinced that they are doing it correctly, start to accuse the others on the team of lifting the hoop, making comments such as, "Who is lifting the hoop?" and "Stop it!" Most teams have to start over quite a few times before they start to address the challenges and take steps to resolve the conflict and attain success.

Tips
- This is a good activity to use before Step by Step to have teams reflect on what it takes to resolve conflict and be successful.
- When you place the hoop on the team's fingers, apply slight downward pressure before letting them begin. This helps create the initial upward pressure that creates the "helium effect."

Variations
The classic version of this game uses a lightweight pole, with the team standing in two lines facing each other. I prefer the hoop because everyone can easily see each other, but using the pole is an option.

Discussion Questions
1. What were some of your initial thoughts regarding this activity?
2. How did your perceptions influence your behavior?
3. How effective was the team at dealing with frustration?
4. Did your team experience any conflict? Why or why not?
5. How was conflict resolved?
6. How did you balance the individual's responsibility with the team's goal?
7. What are some real-life situations that may be similar in nature to this challenge?

Check It Out

Group Size

Any

Materials

One copy of the Checklist Guidelines handout (provided) for each person, index cards, pens

Time

30 to 40 minutes

Procedure

A checklist can serve as a valuable tool for navigating through a conflict. However, to be effective, it needs to be carefully developed, validated, and applied. A checklist clarifies the process and helps team members recall skills as well as important steps. Using a checklist can also enhance objectivity, credibility, and consistency. A checklist provides rational guidelines for the team to follow when emotions may run high.

Have larger groups form into small discussion teams of five to eight participants to develop a step-by-step process to resolve conflict. Use the checklist-building guidelines provided in the handout to assist participants as they create their criteria. They can use the index cards to brainstorm ideas for their list.

Discussion Questions

1. What did you consider as you created your checklist?
2. How did your team's perspective differ from the other teams' perspective?
3. What were you able to learn from the other teams that you may not have considered?
4. How can we use this checklist tool?
5. What are some ways the checklist will improve the manner in which conflict is dealt with?
6. How will we know if it works?

Checklist Guidelines

1. Define the checklist.

☐ Define the checklist's intended uses.

☐ Reflect upon and draw from pertinent training and experience.

☐ Have conversations with other experts.

2. Generate a potential list of checkpoints.

☐ Briefly define each checkpoint.

☐ Add descriptions as needed.

☐ Provide rationale for checkpoints.

☐ Present any warnings for using the checklist.

3. Sort out the checkpoints.

☐ Write each checkpoint on a separate index card.

☐ Decide if any checkpoints can be categorized together or are subsets of another checkpoint.

☐ Review the checkpoints for content and clarity.

☐ Add, subtract, and rewrite checkpoints as needed.

4. Determine the order of the checkpoints.

☐ Decide if an order is important for the intended users.

☐ Provide an ordering of the items on the checklist.

5. Get feedback from potential users.

☐ Ask potential users (other teams) to review and critique the checklist.

☐ Interview the users to get an understanding of their concerns and suggestions.

☐ Take note of any issues that need attention.

6. Revise and finalize the checklist.

☐ Based on the feedback, make any necessary revisions.

☐ Rewrite the items on the checklist.

7. Apply the checklist.

☐ Use the checklist.

☐ Assess its value.

☐ Get additional feedback.

☐ Use feedback to adjust the checklist as needed.

Pins and Needles

OBJECTIVES
- To acknowledge the challenges of incorporating new skills into our everyday lives
- To identify ways to overcome these challenges

Group Size
Any

Materials
Paper, pens

Time
20 to 30 minutes

Procedure

At the conclusion of a confict-resolution training session, acknowledge that making some of the changes required to become more effective at conflict resolution may have participants on pins and needles.

Break large groups into smaller teams of four to seven participants (having at least three small teams works best). Give each person a sheet of paper and have participants write down one thing that is making them nervous or concerned about applying their newfound skills in their everyday lives. Collect the sheets of paper, then shuffle them and pass them out again. Have each small team brainstorm ways to overcome the challenges identified (make sure they write down their ideas on the original paper). After five minutes, have the teams pass their sheets of paper to another team to brainstorm. Three rounds are usually sufficient. Then have the teams present their concerns and solutions to the large group.

Tips

There may be some duplicate concerns, which just proves that we are more alike than we think!

Discussion Questions

1. How do you feel now about your concerns?

2. What insight did you gain by problem-solving your issues?

3. In what way did this activity make you more confident about using your new skills?

2

Communication

Courage is what it takes to stand up and speak.
Courage is also what it takes to sit down and listen.

—Winston Churchill

Communication

You Don't Say

Group Size

Any

Materials

You Don't Say handout (provided) and a table and chair for props

Time

5 to 10 minutes

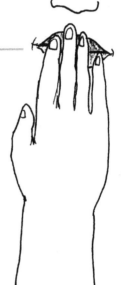

Procedure

Ask for two volunteers to come to the front of the room (or somewhere in the room so the other participants can see them). Let the volunteers know that one of them will be reading aloud some actions while the other person acts them out. After each action, ask for feedback from the group regarding the volunteer's interpretation of the action. After the volunteers finish, give them a big round of applause, making sure to compliment the actor on his or her fine acting abilities, and have them take their seats. Follow with the group discussion.

Variations

Pass out the You Don't Say handout to small teams of five to seven participants and have each team enact the nonverbal signals and their potential meanings. After five minutes ask for their examples, followed by the debriefing discussion.

Discussion Questions

1. How powerful is nonverbal communication?

2. Do we all interpret nonverbal messages in the same way? Why or why not? What is the "correct" interpretation?

3. Based on this activity, what are some things we can keep in mind regarding the messages we send nonverbally?

4. What are some nonverbal signals we may use in times of conflict that adversely affect resolution?

5. What are some nonverbal signals that would indicate a willingness to work toward resolution and collaboration?

You Don't Say

1. Leaning forward in chair

2. Leaning back in chair, arms folded

3. Resting chin in both hands

4. Resting chin on your knuckles

5. Yawning

6. Smiling

7. Frowning

8. Smiling and nodding

9. Rubbing your temples

10. Glancing at watch

11. Looking around the room

12. Tapping fingers on the table

The Way We See It

OBJECTIVES
- To consider the elements of effective listening
- To work together in a creative manner

Group Size

Any

Materials

Flip-chart paper, markers

Time

20 to 40 minutes

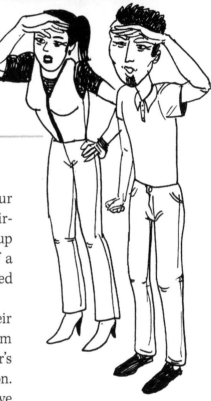

Procedure

Split large groups into smaller teams of four to seven (having at least three teams is desirable). Have each team send a member up to collect their supplies, which consist of a sheet of flip-chart paper and some assorted markers.

Tell the teams that they are to write their definition of *effective listening*. Let them know that you are not looking for Webster's definition, but rather each team's definition. Once each team agrees on a definition, have them write it on their flip-chart paper along with an illustration. After all teams are finished, have the teams present their ideas to the group. Hang up the flip-chart pages on the wall of the room for the duration of the training day.

Tips

Whenever the topic of effective listening comes up throughout the day during your debriefing discussions, refer to these definitions as much as possible.

Discussion Questions

1. What are some barriers to effective listening?

2. How easy or difficult is it to listen in times of conflict? Why?

3. In a conflict situation, how important is the skill of listening?

I'm Listening

Group Size

Any

Materials

One set of the I'm Listening handouts (provided) for each pair

Time

15 to 20 minutes

Procedure

Direct everyone to find a partner and spread out in the room. Give each partnership their two handouts facedown and ask them to keep them facedown until everyone has the handouts. Announce that the activity will be played out in two rounds, Scenario #1 and Scenario #1. Each person will have a specific role to play in each scenario. Each will have the chance to be the talker and the listener. Have them all turn over the handouts at the same time, and give them about a minute to read the directions on the top of their handouts before beginning. After a minute, I usually say, "Now it's time to start talking!" Give them two to three minutes to complete Scenario #1, and then move on to Scenario #2.

Ask the discussion questions, then have partnerships join together (working in groups of four to six) to come up with appropriate listening strategies. After five minutes, have them report back to the entire team.

Tips

Color-code the handouts—Handout A could be green, Handout B could be orange.

Discussion Questions

1. When you were the talker, what feedback did you receive from your listener?

2. How did you feel about that feedback?

3. How did that feedback influence what you said?

4. What are some appropriate listening and feedback strategies?

I'm Listening—Handout A

Directions

Please take a minute to read your script silently. Do not share your script with your partner. When each round begins, you will have 45 seconds to act out your script.

Scenario #1

Talker #1

You are having a very difficult day at work. You've just hung up after talking with an angry customer, your computer is down, and a coworker just snapped at you. It is one of those days when it seems that everything that could possibly go wrong does. You turn to a team member for a little empathy. You just want to talk it out for a few minutes.

Your role: Tell your partner about your difficult day and how you feel.

Scenario #2

Listener #2

One of your colleagues comes to you with good news. You are very busy and preoccupied. Because you have so much going on, you are multitasking— checking your e-mail, texting, looking through the papers on your desk, organizing your workspace, getting up to go make copies, and so on. You don't even have time to look up and make eye contact—after all, if you do, your coworker may keep talking! And you have much more important things to do.

Your role: Use nonverbal feedback to indicate that you don't have time to listen. Everything you do indicates that you are very busy and that your tasks are far more important than taking the time to listen to your coworker.

I'm Listening—Handout B

Directions

Please take a minute to read your script silently. Do not share your script with your partner. When each round begins, you will have 45 seconds to act out your script.

Scenario #1

Listener #1

A team member comes to you with some job-related problems. After listening for a few seconds, you realize that his or her problems are minor compared to yours. You interrupt to negate what your coworker is feeling and to offer your solutions and advice.

Your role: Say things like, "It's no big deal compared to what happened to me . . ."; "Oh, that's nothing, don't worry about it"; "Here is what you need to do"; or "You are making something out of nothing." Interrupt your partner constantly to give your reactions and advice.

Scenario #2

Talker #2

Great news! You just won the lottery! You are so excited that when you get to work you approach the first team member you see to tell him or her all about your good news.

Your role: Tell your partner how this money will change your life, what you plan to do with your winnings, and of course, how happy you are. Be sure to use voice inflection and nonverbal communication to convey your excitement.

Mimes

OBJECTIVES
- To practice questioning and clarification skills
- To learn the skills of dialogue

Group Size

Any

Materials

A list of prepared topic questions displayed so everyone can see them

Time

15 to 20 minutes

Procedure

Many conflicts arise because our assumptions or perceptions are inaccurate. Even though our assumptions may be wrong, we then make judgments based on these inaccurate assumptions. This activity teaches teams the skills of questioning and clarification.

Have everyone find a partner and spread out in the room. Partners can be standing or sitting for this activity. Each team member will get a chance to ask his or her partner a question. Rather than give a verbal answer, the person to whom the question is asked can only mime his or her answer. The asker is invited to ask as many clarification questions as he or she would like to gain an understanding of the other person's answer.

Sample Topic Questions

- When you were a child, how did you like to spend your time?
- What accomplishment are you most proud of?
- If you had a million dollars, what would you do with it?

Discussion Questions

1. How do questioning skills help us understand?

2. In addition to questioning skills, what other skills are necessary to overcome assumptions?

3. What is the value of questioning skills to resolve conflict?

4. What gets in the way of our willingness to ask questions when we are involved in conflict situations?

One Question

OBJECTIVES
- To engage in dialogue
- To practice listening and questioning skills

Group Size

Any

Materials

None

Time

10 to 15 minutes

Procedure

One of the most useful skills in times of conflict is the skill of dialogue. Dialogue can open the door to collaboration. When we engage in dialogue, we keep an open mind, ask questions, and listen to the answers. This activity is a great way to practice those skills.

Have everyone find a partner and a place to sit comfortably. Give participants the criteria for which partner will begin round one (for example, the person with the longest hair, biggest shoes, or darkest eyes). That person begins the round by asking their partner a question. The other person can either just answer the question, or answer and follow up with their own question to continue the dialogue. The challenge is for the partners to see how long they can engage in dialogue using just that one question as a foundation for the conversation. After the topic question, all the additional questions and dialogue have to build on that. Because close-ended questions tend to shut down a conversation, remind your team that questions that begin with *what, where, when, how,* and *why* work best. Here are some examples of opening questions:

- Where did you grow up?
- What do you like about your job?
- Where is one of your favorite vacation spots?
- When did you start working for the company?
- How can you become better at resolving conflict?

To give each partner a chance to ask the topic question, play this game in two rounds.

Tips
The topic question needs to be an open-ended question. It is a good idea to discuss the difference between open- and close-ended questions and ask for some examples before starting (What sports do you like? What are your plans for the summer? What activities are your children involved in at school?).

Discussion Questions
1. What did you notice during the activity?
2. In what ways does it take two to keep the dialogue going?
3. Was this activity more or less challenging than you thought it would be?
4. Did you improve your time during the second round?
5. What did you learn during the first round that allowed you to do that?
6. Do we usually take the time to ask questions when we're in conflict with another? Why or why not?
7. How might asking questions change the course of the conflict?
8. What are some examples of open-ended questions we could use the next time we are in a conflict situation?

Re-Creation

OBJECTIVES

- To improve communication within the team
- To discover the importance of open-ended questions and two-way communication

Group Size

10 to 25

Materials

Multiple sets of identical props

Time

20 to 30 minutes

Procedure

While the instructions are somewhat involved, this game is easy to run. Some preparation and enough space so that your teams can work independently are necessary. You will also need a remote area to display the original model.

Split any large groups into small teams of four or five participants. Depending on your group's size, you will need a different number of supplies. You will need one set of props for each team and one additional set to create the original model. For example, if you plan to have three teams, you will need four of each object (four manuals, four pens, four large paper clips, and four staplers).

Now you are ready to direct your teams. Each team needs two builders, one or two communicators, and one observer. Give each team's builders one identical set of materials and have them station themselves in an area away from the other teams' builders.

Bring your observers to the remote location and have them collaboratively arrange one set of the props. With the example items given, observers could open the manual to page 10, place a stapler across the middle with a pen between the top and bottom of the stapler, and angle a paper clip a specific way on the open page. The observer in each team is the only person who is permitted to see the original model.

Now the game begins as each team's observer walks halfway to the builders' location where the communicators are positioned. The observer tells the communicator(s) all the details he or she can remember about the model. The communicator then goes to the builders to relay the information. The builders, however, can only ask the communicator yes or no questions ("Is the manual open?" "Is it open to page 20?" "Is the stapler on top of the manual?"). When the communicator can't remember any more details, he or she can go back to the observer to talk about the details. The observer can go back to the model as many times as needed.

This goes on until all of the teams feel they have accomplished their goal. Gather everyone together to have them look at the finished models.

Tips
Switch roles and run through the activity a second time to allow for improvements in the process based on the debriefing discussion.

Discussion Questions
1. What did you notice during the activity?
2. What was challenging about the activity?
3. What are some similar challenges we face at work?
4. What plan took shape?
5. How did you make the communication work for you?
6. Communicators, what was your perception?
7. Builders, what was frustrating for you during the activity?
8. Observers, what was your perception?

Pass the Chips

Group Size

Any

Materials

For the facilitator: one copy of the Wright Family Vacation Story handout (provided); for each participant: two poker chips of different colors, one copy of the Wright Family Vacation Questionnaire handout (provided), pen

Time

15 to 20 minutes

Procedure

Have the team form a circle. Pass out the poker chips so that everyone has two different colored chips, holding one in their right hand and one in their left hand. Ask participants to note what chips they are starting with (e.g., one red chip and one white chip). Request that two people standing next to each other have different colored chips. Issue these instructions to your team:

I will be reading a story. When you hear the word right *in the story, all chips get passed once to the right (pass the chip in your right hand to the person on your right and the chip in your left hand to your right hand). When you hear the word* left, *all chips get passed once to the left (pass the poker chip in your left hand to the person on your left and the poker chip in your right hand to your left hand).*

Before beginning, have them shift the poker chips by giving them a practice "right" and "left." Do this a couple times so they are comfortable with the process. Have everyone get their original chips back before starting.

Begin reading the Wright Family Vacation Story handout. Make sure that the participants start to pass their chips beginning with the title of the story (that's essential if they are going to end up with the same chips they started with). Begin reading slowly and then speed up. Don't stop reading or pause to let participants discuss the chip passing. Once the story is finished, have everyone hold out their open hands to show where the chips are. If done accurately, each person should have the same color chips they started with in each hand. Take a few minutes at this point to allow the team to laugh, discuss the process, and evaluate their success.

Now pass out the questionnaire. Give them five minutes to answer the questions. As you go over each question, ask for a show of hands to see how many had the correct answer. Keep track of the number of correct answers for the debriefing discussion.

Tips
You can use assorted coins or small props rather than poker chips.

Discussion Questions
1. What was happening during the poker-chip-passing portion of the activity?
2. What made the activity difficult to accomplish?
3. What impact did other team members have on your ability to keep up with the story and task?
4. How did you feel during the activity?
5. What would have made it easier?
6. How difficult was it to listen and pass the poker chips at the same time?
7. How much of the story do you remember?
8. Was it difficult to answer the questions afterward? What made it difficult?
9. As a team, were you accurate at either task?
10. What can this activity teach us about communication?
11. Do we face similar challenges at work?
12. What are some ways in which these types of challenges lead to communications challenges that may lead to conflict?

Wright Family Vacation Story

Before the Wrights—Mr. and Mrs. Wright and their two children, Cindy and Jeff Wright—left for vacation, they discussed some potential destinations. So no one would be left out or left wanting for a better vacation, they came up with the perfect idea.

Because all the Wrights are left-handed, it made sense that this summer, they would take a trip to London, where the world's largest left-handed store, called Anything Left-Handed, is located. All the Wrights plan to buy one special left-handed item while at the store. Mrs. Wright is getting a can opener, while Mr. Wright is looking for a special left-handed pen to prevent smudges when he writes. Cindy Wright wants a left-handed scissors, and Jeff Wright can't wait to drink coffee out of a left-handed mug.

To the Wrights' surprise, they discovered that Left-Hander's Day is August 13, which is the day they arrive in London. The idea behind Left-Hander's Day is for everyone to celebrate in fun, practical ways, making right-handed family members, friends, and colleagues realize how "dexterous" lefties have to be because they are constantly adapting a right-handed world to work for left-handers. Getting "right-handers" to do everything left-handed for the day is a great way to make the point! After all, the Wrights and other lefties feel they have every right to be left-handed.

Wright Family Vacation Questionnaire

What Do You Remember?

1. How many of the Wrights are left-handed?

_____

2. Where did the Wrights go on vacation?

_____

3. What is the name of the store they planned to visit?

_____

4. What item is Mrs. Wright planning to buy?

_____

5. What beverage will Jeff drink out of his purchase?

_____

6. What day is Left-Hander's Day?

_____

7. How is Left-Hander's Day celebrated?

_____

Keys to Communication

Group Size

6 to 20, split into two, three, or four teams (each team needs at least three participants)

Materials

Painter's tape or rope, three blindfolds for each team, one lock with key per team, one combination lock per team, one slip of paper with all the combinations written out for each team

Time

30 minutes

Procedure

Section off a large area with tape (10 feet by 20 feet is a good size). Instruct the team that this activity is played in three rounds, during which time only blindfolded team members are allowed inside the playing field. For each round, teams will choose a different blindfolded team member. Let the team members know that when they are blindfolded, their team will be guiding them through a simple task.

Round One: Place one blindfolded participant from each team at one end of the playing area. Show everyone else the locks and keys and place them in the center of the playing area (it's best to scatter the items throughout the middle of the area so the team is challenged to find the right key for their lock). The sighted teammates then attempt to verbally (only) tell the blindfolded participants how to find the keys and the lock, and then open the lock.

Round Two: Allow each team three minutes to form a strategy between their teammates and a new blindfolded participant. Then repeat the activity, moving the keys and locks to a new location inside the playing area.

Round Three: Allow for three minutes of strategy, but use a combination lock instead of keys and padlocks. The combination numbers are given to the sighted team members of each team. Only the blindfolded participants can touch the objects, but the combination locks can be brought to their teammates for additional visual assistance during the unlocking procedure (it's best to let them figure this out on their own).

Tips

This can be an indoor or an outdoor activity. Chaos is pretty likely (especially during the first round), so facilitators should stand between the blindfolded participants to make sure they don't bump into each other. It's beneficial to have observers in this activity; they add a great big-picture perspective to the debrief discussion.

Discussion Questions

1. What were some successful and unsuccessful communication techniques used?
2. Were any suggestions made during the strategy sessions that were untried? Why?
3. Were different techniques used for the third round?
4. Did the teams work with or against each other? Why?
5. Blindfolded participants, from your perspective, could your teammates have done anything differently? What would you do differently if you had to do this again?
6. What are some ways we work against each other in the workplace?
7. What did you learn in this activity and how can you apply it at work?

On the Run

- To solve a difficult problem as a team
- To share information
- To overcome frustration and listen effectively

Group Size

Any

Materials

On the Run Instructions, On the Run Clue Cards, On the Run Solution Cards, On the Run Solution handouts (all provided)

Time

20 to 30 minutes

Procedure

Split the group into teams of five to eight. Copy and cut out one set of clue cards and solution cards for each team. Divide the clue cards so each person gets approximately the same number of clues, and have them keep their clues facedown until they get the instructions. Give someone from the team the instructions to read aloud.

After the instructions are read, the team turns over their clues and gets started. At this point, the facilitator can hand out the solution cards so the team can keep track of their solution. Have the team check their answers with the solution handout at the conclusion of the activity.

Discussion Questions

1. What was challenging about this game?

2. Did you experience any conflict during the game? Why or why not?

3. What did your team do well during the activity?

4. What could you have done differently?

5. How difficult was it to listen?

6. What made listening easier?

7. How does it feel as a team to achieve success with a difficult task?

On the Run Instructions

Five friends recently began running together. Each individual in the group has been on an exercise regimen for a different number of months, and they have decided to start running to mix up their routines and add some variety. Each person has noticed a different benefit from working out, but they all agree that they feel great as a result of a healthier lifestyle. From the clues given, can you figure out each person's first and last name, the number of months each has been exercising, the benefit each has experienced, and the brand of athletic shoes each person wears?

You may verbally share the information you have with the other members of your team, but you may not show anyone your clues at any time. Use the solution cards to help track your answers.

Good luck!

On the Run Clue Cards

Copy and cut out the following cards to hand out to your team.

Rico is not the man with the surname Jackson.	Rico doesn't wear Brooks running shoes.
Rico has been exercising for fewer months than the woman with the increased energy level.	The woman with increased energy has been working out for fewer months than the woman who wears Adidas shoes.
The person who has been following a healthy lifestyle for 6 months does not have the surname Walker.	The person who has been working out for the least amount of time is not the man who wears the Mizuno shoes.
The man who wears Saucony shoes has been following his health regimen longer than the person surnamed Lee.	The person surnamed Lee has been following his or her regimen for more months than the person who lowered his or her cholesterol.
The person who has experienced weight loss began his or her regimen at some point after the one who has more muscle tone.	The person who has experienced weight loss began his or her regimen before Heather did.
The Nike shoes are worn by a woman.	Jake is thrilled that he lowered his cholesterol level.
The person surnamed Jackson has not noticed any weight loss.	The woman who has more muscle tone is not Ms. Lee.
Ms. Garcia enjoys running so much that she goes out for a short run at least 5 times a week.	The Adidas shoes are 15 months old and ready to be replaced.

On the Run Solution Cards

Copy and cut out the following cards to hand out to your team.

Solution Cards: Running Shoes

Mizuno	Adidas
Saucony	Brooks
Nike	

Solution Cards: First Names

Heather	Jake
Lucy	Rico
Nick	

Solution Cards: Surnames

Garcia	Walker
Lee	Riley
Jackson	

Solution Cards: Health Benefits

Lower cholesterol	Endurance
Weight loss	Increased energy
Muscle tone	

Solution Cards: Number of Months

3 months	6 months
9 months	12 months
15 months	

On the Run Solution

Jake Jackson, 3 months, lower cholesterol, Brooks shoes

Rico Riley, 6 months, endurance, Mizuno shoes

Heather Lee, 9 months, increased energy, Nike shoes

Nick Walker, 12 months, weight loss, Saucony shoes

Lucy Garcia, 15 months, muscle tone, Adidas shoes

Supply Closet

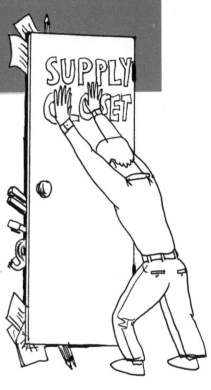

OBJECTIVES
- To improve communication within the team
- To share information for effective problem solving
- To overcome the frustration of working through a challenging task

Group Size

Any

Materials

Supply Closet Instructions, Supply Closet Clue Cards, Supply Closet Solution Cards, Supply Closet Diagram handouts (all provided); pens

Time

20 to 30 minutes

Procedure

Split the group into teams of four to six (more than six and it becomes too difficult for everyone to see and use the diagram during the game). Copy and cut out one set of clue cards and solution cards for each team. Divide the clue cards so each person gets approximately the same number of clues, and have them keep their clues facedown until they get the instructions. Give someone from the team the instructions to read aloud.

After the instructions are read, the team turns over their clues and gets started. The team can use the solution cards and the diagram provided to track their answers. Have the team check their answers with the solution handout at the conclusion of the activity.

Discussion Questions

1. What is challenging when it comes to team problem solving?
2. What is beneficial about working together to solve problems?
3. What did your team do well during the activity?
4. What could you have done differently?
5. How can we use this experience to solve problems more effectively in the workplace?

Supply Closet Instructions

The office supply closet is a mess. In an effort to get organized and maintain consistency, the company issued a diagram to show where each supply is to be stored in the supply closet. The company trainer decided to have some fun with the task and made a team-building game out of the project. Your challenge is to place the correct office supply in the correct position in the closet.

   You may verbally share your information with your team, but you may not show anyone your clues at any time. Use the solution cards and diagram to help track your answers.

   Good luck!

Supply Closet Clue Cards

Copy and cut out the following cards to hand out to your team.

Each column and each horizontal row contains two 1-worded supplies.

Each column and each horizontal row contains two 2-worded supplies.

The two-worded supplies in B3 and C3 each contain the same number of letters.

The supply in B1 is necessary to be able to use the supply in D1.

The paper clips are somewhere higher than the highlighter pens in the same vertical column.

The envelopes are two squares directly below the copy paper.

The envelopes are two squares to the left of the pens.

The tape is located in horizontal row D.

Corner square D4 contains colored paper.

The markers are immediately above the sticky notes in one of the two central vertical columns.

The square containing the staple remover is higher and further to the right than the shipping labels.

Each column and each row contains four different office supplies.

The shipping labels and the staple remover are each either in the same row or the same column as the calculator.

Three of the four supplies in row B begin with the same letter of the alphabet.

The horizontal rows are delegated with the letters A, B, C, and D from top to bottom.

The vertical columns are numbered left to right in order from 1 to 4.

The one-worded supplies in B1 and D1 begin with the same letter of the alphabet.

The staple remover is not in the top row.

The staple remover is in the fourth vertical column.

Supply Closet Solution Cards

Copy and cut out the following cards to hand out to your team.

Calculator	Copy paper
Envelopes	Colored paper
Markers	Paper clips
Pens	Rubber bands
Scissors	Sticky notes
Staples	Staple remover
Stapler	Shipping labels
Tape	Highlighter pens

Supply Closet Diagram

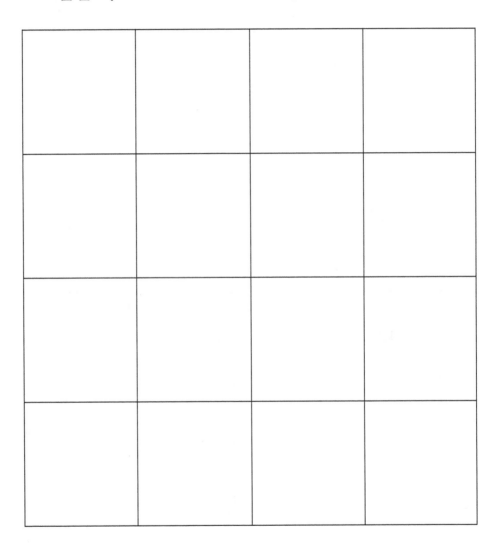

Supply Closet Solution

	1	2	3	4
A	Paper clips	Copy paper	Markers	Scissors
B	Staples	Calculator	Sticky notes	Staple remover
C	Highlighter pens	Envelopes	Rubber bands	Pens
D	Scissors	Shipping labels	Tape	Colored paper

The Butler Did It

Group Size

Any

Materials

The Butler Did It Instructions, The Butler Did It Clue Cards, The Butler Did It Solution Cards, The Butler Did It Solution handouts (all provided)

Time

30 to 40 minutes

Procedure

Split the group into teams of five to eight. Copy and cut out one set of clue cards and solution cards for each team. Divide the clue cards so each person gets approximately the same number of clues, and have them keep their clues facedown until they get the instructions. Give someone from the team the instructions to read aloud.

After the instructions are read, the team turns over their clues and gets started. At this point, the facilitator can hand out the solution cards so the team can keep track of the possible solutions. Have the team check their answers with the solution handout at the conclusion of the activity.

Tips

The last clue (beginning "The six butlers are . . .") is a key clue. If the person who has that clue does not communicate the information clearly, it is likely the team will be unable to solve the problem. If this occurs, it may cause frustrations to build and communication to break down, which can be addressed in the debriefing discussion.

Discussion Questions

1. Why was the communication so challenging?

2. What did you do to overcome those challenges?

3. In what ways did the difficulty level affect your communication?

4. How did you address any conflict that may have occurred?

5. Do difficult challenges sometimes lead to conflict in the workplace?

6. What did you learn in this activity that you could use in similar situations at work?

The Butler Did It Instructions

"Help! Stop! Police!" shouted the bank manager, Mr. Drysdale. "The butler did it!" It took a couple of minutes for the police officer to realize that Mr. Drysdale was speaking the truth. The bank had just been robbed by a man dressed as a butler. Throughout the rest of the day, the police were able to round up six suspects. Each butler had an alibi, so the police had the six come down to the station for a lineup. Mr. Drysdale easily identified the guilty butler and he was locked up behind bars to await his trial. From the clues provided, can you determine the position of each butler in the lineup, where the police found him, and his alibi?

You may verbally share the information you have with the other members of your team, but you may not show anyone your clues at any time. Use the solution cards to help track your answers.

Good luck!

The Butler Did It Clue Cards

Copy and cut out the following cards to hand out to your team.

The culprit is named Jeeves.	Jeeves was found at the antique shop.
The alibi Jeeves gave is that he was at home dusting the Ming vase.	The suspect who claimed to have been home pressing the perfect creases in trousers wasn't found at the café.
The suspect detained at the winery is standing closer to Jeeves than the one detained at the drugstore is standing to Jeeves.	Hobson is not standing next to Jeeves.
Reginald is somewhere to the left of Jeeves.	Godfrey isn't the one who said he was home polishing the silver.

The suspect who claimed to be out having the limo washed and waxed is standing the farthest away from Jeeves.

The suspect who claimed to be out having the limo washed and waxed is standing four to the right of Godfrey.

The suspect found at the bookstore is standing two to the left and two to the right of the ones found at the winery and the drugstore, in some order.

Alfred is standing closer to the suspect found at the drugstore than he is standing to the one found at the cigar shop.

The person who was home drawing a bath while the crime occurred is standing immediately to the right of Reginald.

Hobson was enjoying a croissant when he was found.

There was a shiny limo parked at the drugstore as the police were rounding up the suspects.

The six butlers are (1) Jeeves, (2) the one standing as far to the left of Jeeves as the one found in the café is standing to the right of Jeeves, (3) Lurch, (4) the one who was home pressing the perfect creases in trousers, (5) the one who was home shining shoes, and (6) the one standing three to the left of the one found at the café.

The Butler Did It Solution Cards

Copy and cut out the following cards to hand out to your team.

Solution Cards: Butlers

Reginald	Godfrey
Alfred	Jeeves
Hobson	Lurch

Solution Cards: Locations Found

Cigar shop	Winery
Antique shop	Bookstore
Café	Drugstore

Solution Cards: Alibis

Polishing the silver	Dusting the Ming vase
Drawing a bath	Shining shoes
Pressing the perfect creases in trousers	Having the limo washed and waxed

Solution Cards: Positions in Lineup

Position 1	Position 2
Position 3	Position 4
Position 5	Position 6

The Butler Did It Solution

Position 1, Reginald, cigar shop, polishing the silver

Position 2, Godfrey, winery, drawing a bath

Position 3, Jeeves, antique shop, dusting the Ming vase

Position 4, Alfred, bookstore, pressing the perfect creases in trousers

Position 5, Hobson, café, shining shoes

Position 6, Lurch, drugstore, having the limo washed and waxed

3

Diversity

There never were in the world two opinions alike, no more than two hairs or two grains; the most universal quality is diversity.

—Michel de Montaigne

Another Name Game

Group Size
Any
Materials
None
Time
10 to 20 minutes

Procedure

For an easy way to introduce the concept of diversity, use this in-depth name game. Invite participants to form teams of about four to eight people (the smaller the teams, the less time needed for this activity). Have each person explain the background of his or her name, such as what it means, where it came from, and perhaps the reason his or her parents had for giving that name.

Most people will surprise you with the interesting information behind their name. This can be a rich activity for a diverse team. In fact, the greater the diversity in the team, the more meaningful this activity is.

Variations

- Have groups of 12 or fewer circle up and run this as a single-team activity.
- If time is short, have your group break into twos or threes instead of larger teams.
- After sharing in pairs, ask each person to introduce his or her partner to the team and the story behind the person's name.
- This activity can also be used to reveal the story behind other names, such as nicknames, pets' names, or names of children.

Tips

To ensure greater depth of sharing, use this activity after a warm-up or ice-breaker activity where a certain level of trust has been established within the team.

Discussion Questions

1. How important are names?

2. In what ways does the story behind our names define us?

3. Why is it important to remember and to use names?

4. How does this relate to trust within the team?

5. What are some ways to remember names?

Common Uncommon

- To discover the ways in which we are similar to and different from other team members
- To begin the process of building trust within the team

Group Size
Any

Materials
Paper, pens, or pencils

Time
10 to 20 minutes

Procedure

Split large groups into teams of five to eight people. Give each team a sheet of paper and a pen or pencil. For the first part of the activity, team members find out and write down what they have in common. To make the list, the commonalities must apply to everyone on the team and must be something you could not identify by simply looking at them (we all work at the same place, we all have brown hair, we are all wearing shoes). After five minutes, have someone from each team read their list.

If working with a large group, for the second part of the activity, you can either have half of each smaller team rotate to another team or have participants remain in their original teams. On the back side of the paper, have the team write down what is unique about each team member. That would be something that applies to only one team member (again, going beyond the superficial). Challenge teams to discover at least two things for each person. After seven minutes, have each person say one of the ways in which they are unique.

This is an excellent activity for conflict resolution as it builds awareness that team members have more in common than they may realize. The discovery and recognition of each other's unique characteristics is beneficial as knowledge that we all have something different to offer the team.

Variations

Have participants partner with someone they don't know and discover something they have in common that is not visible. This technique can be used over and over again.

Discussion Questions

1. Were you surprised at how many things you had in common?
2. How does this promote unity on the team?
3. How does discovering commonalities benefit the relationships within the team?
4. How does an awareness of our unique characteristics benefit the relationships within the team?
5. What are some other benefits to the team?
6. How does this influence the level of trust in each other?
7. How does this impact our ability to communicate effectively and resolve conflicts?

Diversity Pays

Group Size
Any

Materials
Diversity Pays handout (provided),
pens, calculator

Time
20 to 30 minutes

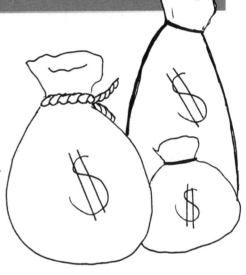

Procedure

This is a great kickoff for the topic of diversity. Split the group into teams of four to six (teams need to have the same number of people). Provide each team with a Diversity Pays handout and have them discuss and award points as instructed on the form. Each team reports their totals to the group at the conclusion of the activity.

Tips

Provide each team with the discussion questions so they can debrief on their own before the group debriefs.

Variations

Take all the team results and average them for a whole-group diversity total.

Discussion Questions

1. What are some ways in which a diverse team can be challenging?

2. What are some ways diversity benefits the team?

3. Are we always rewarded for our differences? If not, why? If so, in what ways?

4. How does team diversity contribute to conflict?

5. How does team diversity contribute to collaboration?

6. What can we do to promote diversity in our team?

Diversity Pays

Award each team member 1 point for each base category that applies to him or her. Bonus points are awarded in addition to the base category points. For example, if every member of a team of five is born in a different state and one team member is born in a different country, the team gets 5 base points plus 5 bonus points for a total of 10 points for the category.

Base Category	Base Point Value	Team Base Points	Bonus Category	Bonus Point Value	Team Bonus Points	Total of Columns 3 + 6
Each different birth month	1		Born on a holiday	3		
Each different birth state or country	1		Born in a different country	5		
Each different eye color	1		Green eyes	2		
Each sibling	1		No siblings Twins Triplets	3 5 10		
Each continent visited (not just a stopover)	1		For visiting 5 For visiting 7	10 15		
Each language spoken fluently	1		Sign language 3+ languages	5 10		

Base Category	Base Point Value	Team Base Points	Bonus Category	Bonus Point Value	Team Bonus Points	Total of Columns 3 + 6
Each different musical instrument played	1		3+ instruments Played professionally	5 7		
Each year married	1		10+ years (to one person) 20+ years (to one person)	5 10		
Each living parent	1		Grandparent Great-grandparent	3 5		
Each state lived in	1		Different country lived in	5		
Each different job	1		10 + years in one job 20+ years in one job	5 10		
For visiting the following: Grand Canyon, Pyramids of Giza, Eiffel Tower, Taj Mahal, Great Wall of China, Stonehenge, Great Barrier Reef	1		For visiting 3+ For visiting 5+ For visiting all 7	5 10 15		
Total						

It's Classified

Group Size

Any

Materials

None

Time

10 to 20 minutes

Procedure

Split large groups into teams of six to 10 people. Then give the following instructions to the teams:

> We all tend to classify and stereotype each other. Usually this type of classification is subjective, unhelpful, and can be unfair and discriminatory.
>
> The challenge is to discover three ways to classify yourselves into two, three, or four subgroups in a way that each subgroup contains approximately the same number of people. The number of subgroups will depend on the size of the team. Subgroups must contain at least two team members. The criteria used to classify can contain only positive characteristics.
>
> Examples of criteria that could be used to divide or classify the team include the types of foods we like, the different hobbies we enjoy, or our favorite ways to exercise. However, be creative and think of your own ideas rather than using these examples.

Tips

You can start with a simple fifty-fifty split, which is the fastest and easiest. Once they have the idea, allow the teams some flexibility to classify themselves into additional subgroups.

Discussion Questions

1. What did it take to find out and think about each other in different ways?

2. What makes a classification positive/helpful rather than negative/prejudicial?

3. How does this affect the interactions and contributions of team members?

4. How does this influence our ability to collaborate?

5. How can this experience help us in the workplace?

In or Out?

Group Size

10 to 25

Materials

Assorted objects in a bag,
In or Out? handout, pens

Time

10 to 15 minutes

Procedure

To prepare for this activity, gather together a variety of objects that can easily be categorized in groups (five playing cards, five balls, or five paper clips). You will also need two items that cannot be categorized with the others (one pen and one staple remover). Place in a bag the same number of items as team members. For example, for a team of 15 participants, you could place in a large bag: five playing cards, four balls, four pens, one paper clip, and one ruler.

As team members come back from a break, have them pick an object out of the bag. After everyone has something, invite them to group together according to their items. The two team members who have the "odd" items will either stand uncomfortably or decide to team up. Go through the motions of trying to help them find their teams. It may be a little uncomfortable, which is natural. If teams offer to include them, hold off just a bit to make sure they don't belong somewhere else (which they don't). It's all part of the activity. You want it to be noticeable that they don't have a team, but you don't want it to go on too long.

It will also be interesting to notice the lengths that some teams will go through to include them in their team. If this happens, be sure to use this in the debriefing discussion.

Thank the two members and have them join a team. Pass out the In or Out? handout to each team member. Allow each person five to 10 minutes to complete Parts 1 and 2 on the handout, then form small discussion groups to answer the last two questions in Part 3 on the handout. Follow with a group debriefing using the discussion questions below.

Tips
There is some risk involved with this game, so it's best to incorporate this activity after some icebreakers and climate-setting activities where a certain level of trust has been established within the team.

Discussion Questions
1. What did you notice as everyone tried to find where they belonged?
2. What effect does it have on the team whether team members feel included or excluded?
3. For the two of you who did not "belong," what was your experience like?
4. For those of you who were included in teams, how did you feel when two of your team members did not belong anywhere?
5. What can team members do or say to help create the feeling of inclusion?
6. What can the team leader do to help promote inclusion within the team?

In or Out?

Part 1. Identify a Time When You Felt Included in a Group
What happened to make you feel included?

_____

_____

What was the impact on your behavior?

_____

_____

How did this impact the team?

_____

_____

Part 2. Identify a Time When You Felt Excluded from a Group
What happened to make you feel excluded?

_____

_____

What was the impact on your behavior?

_____

_____

How did this impact the team?

_____

_____

Part 3. Team Debriefing Questions

What can team members do or say to help create the feeling of inclusion?

_____

_____

What can the team leader do to help promote inclusion within the team?

_____

_____

Take a Walk

Group Size
  Any
Materials
  None
Time
  10 to 15 minutes

Procedure

Have participants pair up. Each partnership stands face to face and a comfortable distance (about three feet) apart to begin. Tell them they will be discussing the ways in which they are different from, and similar to, their partner. As they discover a difference, they must move a step away from each other. As they discover a similarity, have them move a step closer.

Tips

The differences are usually things we can see, such as hair color, height, age, and so on. The similarities are often things that have to do with characteristics, preferences, and personality, which require more conversation and questions to discover.

Discussion Questions

1. How far apart did you get before you looked for some similarities?
2. How close did you get before you looked for more differences?
3. Why is it important to balance the two?
4. How does a team benefit from a balance of the two?
5. What did you notice about your differences?
6. When do differences in people in a group prevent reaching certain objectives?
7. How do these differences strengthen the group as a whole?
8. What would this group be like if there were very few differences in people? How would you feel if this were so?
9. What did you notice about your similarities?
10. How do our similarities help build trust within our team?

What a Bunch of Characters

Group Size

Any

Materials

Two copies of the What a Bunch of Characters handout (provided) for each team, slips of paper, pens

Time

20 to 30 minutes

Procedure

Split large groups into smaller teams of four to seven participants (having at least three teams is desirable). Ask each team to come up with three well-known "characters" and to write each name on its own slip of paper. The characters can be real or imaginary, alive or dead, famous, but no criminals, please. Tell them that, ideally, the characters should have distinctive personalities. Some examples are Mr. Rogers, the Incredible Hulk, Oprah, Donald Trump, George Carlin, Superman, Chris Rock, Gandhi, Einstein, Judge Judy, James Bond, Rocky, Harry Potter, Darth Vader, or Lucy (from Peanuts).

Collect all the slips of paper, then have each team choose two from the bunch and complete a handout for each character. After 15 minutes, ask teams to report what they learned from their characters.

Variations

The facilitator can create the character slips in advance.

Discussion Questions

1. Which characters handle conflict the most effectively? In what ways are they effective?

2. Which characters don't handle conflict well? What do they do that's ineffective?

3. What are some techniques we can learn from our characters to help us resolve conflict?

4. What are some weaknesses we can be aware of?

5. What are some things we can teach our characters?

What a Bunch of Characters

Name of Character

_____

Qualities

_____

Strengths

_____

Weaknesses

_____

1. How does your character typically handle conflict?

_____

_____

2. What strengths above contribute to your character's ability to resolve conflict?

_____

_____

3. What weaknesses above hinder your character's ability to resolve conflict?

_____

_____

4. What can you learn from your character that would improve your ability to resolve conflict?

_____

_____

5. What could you teach your character to help him or her become more effective at resolving conflict?

_____

_____

4

Trust

Few things help an individual more than to place responsibility upon him, and to let him know that you trust him.

—Booker T. Washington

Two Truths and a Lie— with a Twist!

Group Size

Any

Materials

A copy of the Two Truths and a Lie Team Discussion Questions handout (provided)

Time

15 to 20 minutes

Procedure

For this new twist on a classic activity, start by breaking large groups into small discussion teams of four or five participants. Tell the teams that, one by one, team members should tell the others on their team two truths and one lie about themselves. As each person is talking, the role of other team members is to listen. After the team has heard everyone's "facts," start with the first person and have team members guess what information was a lie and why they chose that item as the untruth. After everyone has had a chance to guess, ask teams to answer the discussion questions.

Tips

The *why* part of the guessing is the new twist and what makes this classic activity perfect for a discussion on how we form judgments and how we base our interactions and actions on these judgments, whether they are accurate or not. These judgments become the filters through which we listen. Prejudging stands in the way of effective listening, which is a necessary skill for conflict resolution.

Discussion Questions

1. What were your guesses based on?
2. Were any of your guesses based on preexisting judgments?
3. Does this ever happen when you are interacting with someone else?
4. Why does this happen? What can we do about it?
5. In what ways does this affect our communication?
6. How does this impact our ability to resolve conflict?

Two Truths and a Lie Team Discussion Questions

1. What criteria did you use to make your guesses?

_____

_____

2. How did preexisting judgments affect your guesses?

_____

_____

3. In what ways do these preexisting judgments influence our communication?

_____

_____

4. Please discuss some examples from your experience when inaccurate judgments contributed to ineffective communication.

_____

_____

5. How might this impact our ability resolve conflict?

_____

_____

Five and Five

Group Size

Up to 20

Materials

Index cards or slips of paper, pens

Time

15 to 20 minutes

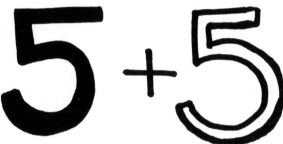

Procedure

Ask everyone to write down five of their likes and five of their dislikes on an index card or slip of paper. Collect all the cards and read them aloud one at a time. The goal for the team is to guess what card goes with which person.

Discussion Questions

1. How well do you know the members of your team?
2. Were you surprised by any of the likes or dislikes?
3. How comfortable were you sharing this type of information?
4. What are some ways an activity such as this improves our working relationships?
5. What are some ways this can build trust?

Single File

OBJECTIVES
- To build trust
- To practice dialogue skills
- To understand that there may be more than one "right" answer

Group Size
Up to 20 works best

Materials
List of extremes

Time
20 to 40 minutes

Procedure

Have the team stand up and gather together. To get them in the spirit of the activity, have them line up shoulder-to-shoulder, from shortest to tallest —one extreme to the other. Stress that the one requirement in the game is that the team needs to arrange themselves in a single-file line. If two people appear to be the same height, they have to figure out the correct order.

Now that they have the idea, let them know you will be calling out other extremes. The team members have to figure out where in the single-file line is an accurate representation of their thoughts and feelings regarding the topic in question.

Call out the first set of extremes by saying that "I make decisions with my gut" is the extreme to the left and "I use logic to make decisions" is the extreme to the right. Now observe as the team figures out the order that is a correct representation of their position on the topic. Refrain from offering any assistance other than reminding the team that they must have a single-file line.

Once they are in line, either ask a few mid-activity questions, or call out the next set of extremes. Usually about five to seven sets is a good number. Begin with safer topics and move on to more in-depth extremes.

List of Extremes

- I make decisions with my gut. / I use logic to make decisions.
- I like to jump into action. / I prefer to watch and wait.
- I stand firm on my decisions. / I look for ways to compromise.
- I like to compete. / I like to collaborate.
- I like to take risks. / I like to stay within my comfort zone.
- I believe you need to look at the big picture. / I believe you must pay attention to the details.
- I prefer to avoid conflict. / I prefer to confront conflict.
- I like to act spontaneously. / I like to plan everything out.
- I keep my eye on the goal. / I pay attention to the process.
- I express my frustrations. / I keep my emotions to myself.
- I like no surprises. / I embrace the unexpected.

Tips

Don't allow a tie—remind them that the line must be single file.

Mid-Activity Discussion Questions

If using the first two topics on the extremes list, which are similar and build a level of comfort with the process, wait to ask the mid-activity questions after the second topic and while the team is still in line.

1. Looking around at your team, are there surprises regarding the positions in line?
2. What techniques can we use to determine positions as we move thorough additional topics?
3. Which positions will likely require the most discussion?
4. How does this process build trust within the team?

Discussion Questions

Some possible answers are included in parentheses.

1. Which spots are the easiest to decide on? Why? *(usually the extremes)*
2. Which spots are the most difficult? Why? *(middle spots; more gray area)*
3. How did you figure out your place in line? *(how I related to those around me; asked questions to understand the perspective of those around me)*
4. How did you feel if/when someone else pressured you into switching your spot? *(frustrated, like they were trying to think for me)*
5. If you were able to decide quickly where you stood on any of the issues, how did you react when it took some people much longer? *(impatient; doesn't everyone know their own mind?)*
6. Were you surprised to see so many different perspectives? So many similar perspectives?
7. In times of conflict, do we sometimes assume that our opponent is our extreme opposite? How likely is this assumption? If this is our assumption, how might this influence the outcome?
8. How can we more accurately assess another person's perspective? *(engage in dialogue)*

Words of Wisdom

Group Size

Any

Materials

Words of Wisdom Quiz and Answer Key handouts (all provided) for each team, pens

Time

20 to 30 minutes

Procedure

Tell the team that they are going to have a chance to find out what some of the great minds in history had to say about conflict. Some of the quotes on the handout are accurate; some are inaccurate. Their job is to come to a consensus as to which are real and which are not. Have them use the "Consensus Thumbs" technique described at the end of this chapter to determine if they have agreement.

Divide the group into small teams of four to seven people. Provide a quiz handout to each team. Suggest that while many of the quotations are verbatim, this does not mean that there are not other valid and conflicting points of view. After 15 minutes, go over the discussion questions with the entire group.

Tips

After they have completed the quiz, pass out the answer key to the small teams to check their answers and continue to discuss their thoughts for an additional five minutes prior to the group discussion.

Variations

Have teams come up with their own quotation after discussing those on the handout.

Discussion Questions

1. Has your perspective on conflict changed? What caused you to change your mind?
2. Did your perspective differ from some of the great minds?
3. Are there any you disagree with? Explain.
4. What did this activity teach you?
5. Which quote reflects your thoughts about conflict?
6. In what ways has your perspective on conflict changed since the beginning of this game?

Words of Wisdom Quiz

Some of these quotations are word-for-word statements and some of them have been changed. What do you think? As a team, you have 15 minutes to discuss the statements and come to a consensus as to which quotes are real and which are not.

1. The opposite of a profound truth may well be another profound truth.

True _____ False _____

2. The truth is that our finest moments are most likely to occur when we are feeling deeply uncomfortable, unhappy, or unfulfilled. For it is only in such moments, propelled by our discomfort, that we are likely to step out of our ruts and start searching for different ways or truer answers.

True _____ False _____

3. Whenever two good people argue over principles, they are both wrong.

True _____ False _____

4. Listening is waiting to talk.

True _____ False _____

5. I've found that I can only change how I act if I stay aware of my beliefs and assumptions. Thoughts always reveal themselves in behavior.

True _____ False _____

6. Human beings love to be right. When a person is willing to give up being right, a whole world of possibilities opens up.

True _____ False _____

7. If you're listening, you're not learning.

True _____ False _____

8. Life is ninety percent what happens to me and ten percent how I react to it.

True _____ False _____

9. Creativity comes from a collaboration of ideas.

True _____ False _____

10. Have you learned lessons only of those who admired you, and were tender with you, and stood aside for you? Have you not learned the great lessons of those who rejected you, and braced themselves against you?

True _____ False _____

Words of Wisdom Answer Key

1. True—"The opposite of a profound truth may well be another profound truth."
—Niels Bohr

2. True—"The truth is that our finest moments are most likely to occur when we are feeling deeply uncomfortable, unhappy, or unfulfilled. For it is only in such moments, propelled by our discomfort, that we are likely to step out of our ruts and start searching for different ways or truer answers."
—M. Scott Peck

3. False—"Whenever two good people argue over principles, they are both right."
—Marie von Ebner-Eschenbach

4. False—"Listening is not waiting to talk."
—Scott Ginsberg

5. True—"I've found that I can only change how I act if I stay aware of my beliefs and assumptions. Thoughts always reveal themselves in behavior."
—Margaret Wheatley

6. True—"Human beings love to be right. When a person is willing to give up being right, a whole world of possibilities opens up."
—Pete Salmansohn

7. False—"If you're not listening, you're not learning."
—Lyndon B. Johnson

8. False—"Life is ten percent what happens to me and ninety percent how I react to it."
—Charles Swindoll

9. False—"Creativity comes from a conflict of ideas."
—Donatella Versace

10. True—"Have you learned lessons only of those who admired you, and were tender with you, and stood aside for you? Have you not learned the great lessons of those who rejected you, and braced themselves against you?"
—Walt Whitman

Word Search

Group Size

Any

Materials

Word Search Example, Word Search #1, Word Search #2, and Word Search Score Sheet/Discussion handouts (all provided), one for each team; paper and pens for each person; clipboard and calculator (both optional) for each team

Time

20 to 30 minutes

Procedure

Break your group into teams of six to eight participants. Ask one person from each team to volunteer to act as the team observer and come up to get the team supplies. Each team should be given blank paper and pens and a copy of the four handouts. Have the observer distribute the blank paper and pens to his or her teammates.

Tell the teams that when the activity begins, the observer is going to show them a word search puzzle similar to the example on the handout (have observers hold up the Word Search Example handout or display it on a clipboard). Let them know they will have one minute to look at the puzzle and find and write down as many words as possible. This is to be done silently and individually, so they may not work with anyone else on the team. The observer is not an active player.

To begin the game, have the observers display Word Search #1 for one minute and then take it down (the facilitator keeps time and will be starting and ending each round). Give individuals a moment to finish writing down any last-minute words. Team members are awarded one point for each correct word. Have each person total his or her words. The puzzle can be presented again at this time for team members to verify correct words.

Ask the observers to add the individual scores together and divide by the number of people on the team to get a team average. The observer records this number under Individual Score on the score sheet.

Next, have the team members count how many words they got as a group. This is the total of all the different words discovered by the team. If anyone on the team got a correct word, it is counted, but only once. The observer records this number under Group Score on the score sheet.

Now tell the group that in a moment, the observer will show them a different word search puzzle that will contain new words. This time the team can collaborate, strategize, and talk throughout the round. Give the teams a two-minute planning session before the round begins. Allow them to look at Word Search #1 to assist their planning. At the end of two minutes (or when the talking dies down), give the teams the go-ahead to begin. Have the observers present Word Search #2 for one minute and then take it down. Allow two minutes for the team to discuss and add any last-minute words based on the words discovered. (For example, if one team member found the word *together*, someone else on the team may realize that additional words could be *to*, *get*, *got*, *her*, and *he*.)

Have the team count the correct words using the puzzle as a reference. The observers record this number under Team Score. Give the teams 10 minutes to complete the questions on the score sheet then follow with the group discussion.

Variations

Make your own word search puzzle based on your team, theme, industry, and company.

Discussion Questions

1. Did you notice an improvement between the two rounds?

2. Why was there such an improvement?

3. Observers, what differences did you notice between the two rounds?

4. What is the difference between working individually, as a group, and as a team?

5. What makes an effective team?

6. In what ways does collaboration benefit the team? The company? The customers?

7. Did you have the impression you were in competition with the other teams? If so, did you guard your answers?

8. Is there a possibility that any other teams were able to find additional words? If so, what could we have done differently to see the full effects of collaboration?

9. How can we collaborate more easily at work?

Word Search Example

This is an example of a word search puzzle (the words are in bold print).

S	X	R	S	**D**	D	**E**	X	**I**	B	E	V
I	V	E	**R**	P	**X**	P	**L**	**S**	C	Z	**A**
H	U	**O**	T	**A**	M	F	G	**Z**	Q	L	V
T	**W**	I	**M**	Y	A	V	I	Y	**Z**	H	P
R	M	**P**	M	W	G	U	P	K	**F**	**U**	T
A	**L**	Q	N	Z	O	M	R	**O**	W	U	**P**
E	O	V	S	P	G	**H**	**C**	**R**	**A**	**E**	**S**
K	Z	Y	I	R	N	U	M	C	**N**	C	Q

Word Search #1

```
G  E  C  K  O  T  N  C  U  T  A  C
R  T  O  A  D  E  O  N  H  S  I  F
A  A  F  N  L  V  I  P  E  R  G  F
U  P  N  G  M  C  L  I  A  U  Q  P
G  E  A  A  O  G  O  H  T  R  A  W
A  E  S  R  U  B  E  A  R  N  A  Q
J  H  N  O  S  G  Q  J  D  O  G  T
H  S  A  O  E  K  I  A  R  B  E  Z
```

Word Search #2

```
B  E  A  R  E  S  O  O  G  Q  A  N
N  C  M  V  A  Q  M  S  D  U  N  E
R  O  A  D  R  U  N  N  E  R  T  T
E  X  L  M  S  A  G  A  E  E  E  T
G  O  L  K  E  I  P  A  R  A  A  I
I  F  R  U  F  L  O  W  J  G  T  K
T  A  R  E  H  T  N  A  P  L  E  A
T  O  C  E  L  O  T  U  M  E  R  Y
```

Word Search Score Sheet/Discussion

Individual Score	Group Score	Team Score

Team Discussion Questions

1. Did you notice an improvement between the two rounds?

2. Why was there such an improvement?

3. Observers, what differences did you notice between the two rounds?

4. What is the difference between working individually, as a group, and as a team?

5. What makes an effective team?

6. In what ways does collaboration benefit the team? The company? The customers?

7. Did you have the impression you were in competition with the other teams? If so, did you guard your answers?

8. Is there a possibility that any other teams were able to find additional words? If so, what could we have done differently to see the full effects of collaboration?

9. How can we collaborate more easily at work?

Rock and Roll

Group Size

6 to 16

Materials

One Rock and Roll Score Sheet
and one Rock and Roll Point
Sheet (all provided); one Rock
and Roll Player Instructions,
Rock card, and Roll card (all provided) for each team; tape; two
clipboards; paper; pens

Time

30 to 60 minutes

Procedure

While there is a lengthy description for this game, it is not challenging to facilitate. This is a game you would want to practice with some family or friends before taking it live. After practicing this game, you will see that it is not difficult to play, but the game depends on the rules being respected and followed by both teams.

Split the group into two teams of three to eight, Team A and Team B. (Teams do not have to have the exact same number of people.) If you have more than 16 people in your group, additional team members can act as observers (up to three observers are plenty). Say to the teams, "The object of this game is to win, and the way to win is to accumulate the maximum positive points possible." The facilitator can repeat this any number of times so it really sinks in. The wording needs to be precise (interpretation comes into play here and can be discussed later in the debriefing discussion).

Tape the Score Sheet and Point Sheet on the wall so both teams can see them. Invite the teams to read the Player Instructions and let them know that the rules need to be followed specifically to play the game with integrity. After the teams have a few minutes to read the instructions, direct them to begin the voting process to decide as a team whether they will show "rock" or "roll." When the teams are ready, have them place their voting card on the clipboard and hold it facedown. The facilitator then says, "1, 2, 3, show!" and the teams hold up their cards. At the end of each round, the facilitator tallies the points and records them so everyone can see the results.

Give teams two to five minutes between rounds to discuss and vote. As the rounds go on, you may need to give them more time as some on the team may begin to see the scoring benefit of working with the other team and try to convince the others on their team to vote a certain way to maximize the total score. As this new way of thinking unfolds, be sure to enforce the rule that teams cannot speak to each other. After five rounds, record the total points (adding Team A and Team B together).

Tips

Having observers to help enforce the rules is a good idea. You want the teams to be far enough apart that they cannot overhear each other to get any insight as to how the other team is voting.

This game is similar to Super Stars in Chapter 7. In both games, cooperation and trust wins and blind pursuit of self-interest loses.

Variations

You can make this work with larger groups by using some of your participants as facilitators. For each group of 16, have two team members act as team facilitators to tally the votes, enforce the rules, and observe the activity. You could do a facilitator brief for a couple of minutes as they come up to get the supplies for their teams. Provide an additional copy of the rules for the team facilitators.

Discussion Questions

1. What did you notice during the game?
2. Were any of you frustrated with your team's voting decisions? Why?
3. What are some limitations of "majority rules" as a way for a team to make decisions? Is there a better way? What is that?
4. Did your strategy change along the way?
5. How did you interpret "The object of this game is to win, and the way to win is to accumulate the maximum positive points possible"?
6. How did your interpretation affect your team's vote?
7. In what ways did trust come into play?
8. Why did your team decide to take a risk (showing "roll" for a lower individual score) and trust the other team would follow? What prevented you from taking that risk (if you didn't)?
9. What happened when the other team did not react the way you hoped they would?
10. In what ways does competition lead to conflict? What other options do we have?
11. How can you implement the lessons learned here into your workplace?

Rock and Roll
Player Instructions

- Each team receives one Rock card and one Roll card.
- The object of the game is to win. The way to win is to accumulate the maximum positive points possible.
- Any communication between the two teams is prohibited (this includes verbal and nonverbal communication).
- A team voting session takes place before each round, but it is important that the other team not see the vote before "showtime" when the facilitator will ask both teams to reveal the card that reflects their vote for that round.
- Every person on the team must vote either Rock or Roll.
- Majority rules as the team's vote.
- When both teams are ready, the facilitator will count "1, 2, 3, show," at which time both teams will show either a Rock or a Roll card.
- Facilitator will compute team scores according to the Point Sheet.
- Play is same for all rounds.
- Breaking any of these rules may result in the termination of the game, so please play fair.

Rock and Roll Score Sheet

Round	Team A	Team B
1		
2		
3		
4		
5		

Total Points

Rock and Roll Point Sheet

Points	Team A Shows	Team B Shows	Points
+5	Rock	Roll	−5
−5	Roll	Rock	+5
−3	Rock	Rock	−3
+3	Roll	Roll	+3

Rock

Roll

Consensus Thumbs

Group Size
Any
Materials
None
Time
5 minutes

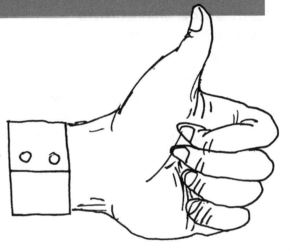

Procedure

This is a technique rather than a game and can be used at the conclusion of a problem-solving activity such as The Two Men in Chapter 5. Before the team makes their final answer, they ask for a show of thumbs to see how comfortable everyone is with the solution. Explain that one team member will present the solution to be decided upon. After the solution is presented, there will be a show of thumbs to indicate each team member's opinion. There are three options:

- Thumbs up: "I am comfortable and confident in the decision."
- Thumbs sideways: "I have some reservations, but if the team decides on this course of action, I will support the team and this decision."
- Thumbs down: "I am uncomfortable with this solution and need to discuss it further." (Thumbs down simply means that there's more to talk about.)

After a show of thumbs, follow up with any more discussion or move forward with the decision.

Tips

Using a majority-rules technique may force some on the team to go along to get along, even if they disagree with the decision. The majority-rules technique may take less time, but the team attitude is more positive when you strive for consensus. The Consensus Thumbs technique is a great way for everyone to be heard in a nonthreatening manner.

Discussion Questions

1. Why is building consensus important?

2. What is the benefit to the Consensus Thumbs technique?

3. What did you like about the technique?

4. How do you as a team feel about your decision?

5. In what ways might this be a time saver for a team?

6. In what situations could you use this technique?

5

Perspective

People are disturbed not by things, but by the view they take of them.

—*Epictetus*

In Character

OBJECTIVES

- To understand another's perspective
- To experience true dialogue
- To learn how to listen without judging
- To develop a deeper level of trust

Group Size

Any

Materials

A list of topics displayed so everyone can see them

Time

15 to 20 minutes

Procedure

Have participants pick partners and choose a topic from the topic list. Encourage participants to choose a pair of topics where they have preexisting and opposite viewpoints. One person takes one viewpoint regarding the topic; the other person takes the opposing viewpoint. For example, one person believes the toilet paper should roll over the top while the other believes the paper should roll from the bottom.

Once a topic is agreed upon and it has been decided which partner will take which side of the argument, give them their objective. Let participants know they will need to gain a thorough understanding of each other's viewpoint because eventually each partner will take on the other person's role—the role that is opposite from his or her own position. To play the other role convincingly, have participants interview each other so they can really get into character when it comes time to play the role of the opposing viewpoint. Emphasize that you will be expecting them to make us believe their character.

The interviews are the activity. In learning how to play their role convincingly, they are more likely to be open and curious. To role-play with sincerity, they will have to suspend their beliefs and seek to understand their partner's viewpoint. In the process of learning to play a different role, they will have engaged in dialogue. Allow ten minutes for the interviews, then begin the debrief discussion.

Sample Topic Ideas

- Toilet paper should roll from the top/toilet paper should roll from the bottom
- Glass half full/glass half empty
- Night person/morning person
- Coke/Pepsi
- Tuck/untuck (sheets)
- Mustard or ketchup
- Mac or PC
- Dogs or cats

Tips

When coming up with additional topic ideas, it's best to keep the topics light and fun.

Discussion Questions

1. When you were asking questions to research your part, how well did you listen?
2. What listening skills did you use?
3. How was this listening different from the way we usually listen?
4. What kind of feedback did you provide when listening?
5. When we have opposite beliefs, do we usually take the time to understand the other person's viewpoint? Why not?
6. What did it feel like to engage in dialogue? Where can we use this skill?
7. In what ways might dialogue transform conflict?

The Usual Suspects

OBJECTIVES

- To experience how different perspectives can lead to accusations and conflict
- To understand that the team's behavior is the responsibility of the whole team

Group Size

Up to 20

Materials

None

Time

10 to 20 minutes

Procedure

Have everyone stand up and arrange themselves in one big circle. The game begins with the facilitator pointing at someone across the circle and saying, "Hey, you," holding that position. That person now points to someone across the circle and says, "Hey, you," and keeps pointing. Continue the "Hey, you" until everyone on the team is pointing to someone else. The last participant points back at the facilitator with a final "Hey, you" to complete the cycle. Before everyone drops their hands, ask the participants to remember who their point person is.

The facilitator starts again with a "Hey, you" to his or her point person, but in this round, instead of pointing, the facilitator simply stares at the point person, holding that position. That person now says, "Hey, you," and stares at his or her point person, and so on until the cycle comes back to the facilitator.

By now, everyone should have their eyes focused on their point person. Explain to the team that their objective is to keep their eyes fixed on their point person and copy their every move. Ask the team to stand completely still for the duration of the activity. No one is allowed to move unless his or her point person moves. Whatever movements the point person makes must be copied exactly by the person fixed on him or her. No other movements are allowed. Start the game and let it go until there are some obvious movements. Say, "Hey, wait a minute, who is moving? We are supposed to stand still. Let's try that again." Begin the game again and let it go until the movements take over. Go right into the discussion questions.

Discussion Questions

1. What happened to the idea of standing still? Who moved?

2. Do we all have the same perspective of the situation?

3. How common is it to assign guilt? Why?

4. When a team is working toward a goal, how effective is the "blame game"?

5. In what ways does this contribute to conflict?

6. Does this ever happen at work? What can we do instead?

Resolutions

Group Size

Any

Materials

One copy of the Resolutions, Face Your Fears, or Most Common Words handout (all provided) for each person, pens

Time

35 to 45 minutes

Procedure

Provide each participant with a copy of the Resolutions handout. Ask participants to rank the top 10 New Year's resolutions in order from most to least popular. No discussion is allowed at this point in the activity. After about four minutes, have teams of five to eight discuss their individual rankings and come up with a team consensus ranking (an option is to use the Consensus Thumbs technique described in Chapter 4). The team has 10 minutes to reach a decision.

Compare the individual and team results with the answer key below.

Answers for Resolutions

1. Spend time with loved ones
2. Get fit/eat right
3. Lose weight
4. Stop smoking
5. Enjoy life more/reduce stress
6. Stop drinking
7. Manage debt/save money
8. Get a better education/learn something new
9. Be more charitable/help others
10. Become more organized

Tips

Request that, in the spirit of the game, no one uses technology to their advantage by simply googling the answers.

Variations

Instead of the Resolutions handout, use the Face Your Fears or Most Common Words handouts (provided). The answers are provided below.

Answers for Face Your Fears

1. Snakes
2. Public speaking
3. Heights
4. Confined spaces
5. Spiders and insects
6. Needles and getting shots
7. Mice
8. Flying on a plane
9. Dogs
10. Thunder and lightning

Answers for Most Common Words

1. The
2. Of
3. To
4. And
5. A
6. In
7. Is
8. It
9. You
10. That

Discussion Questions

1. What differences did you notice between the two methods (individual versus collaboration)?
2. Were all ideas heard? Why or why not?
3. In what ways does the team benefit from diverse perspectives?
4. What method gave you a more effective result?
5. What are the challenges of collaboration?
6. What are the benefits of collaboration?

Resolutions

Most of us make New Year's resolutions every January. Here is a list of the most common resolutions. Your task is to order the resolutions from most popular (number 1) to least popular (number 10) according to Listverse.com.

New Year's Resolution	Individual Ranking	Team Ranking
A. be more charitable/help others	_____	_____
B. become more organized	_____	_____
C. enjoy life more/reduce stress	_____	_____
D. get fit/eat right	_____	_____
E. get a better education/learn something new	_____	_____
F. lose weight	_____	_____
G. manage debt/save money	_____	_____
H. spend time with loved ones	_____	_____
I. stop drinking	_____	_____
J. stop smoking	_____	_____

Face Your Fears

Most of us have fears and anxiety regarding certain things. Here is a list of the most common fears of Americans. Your task is to order the fears from most common (number 1) to least common (number 10) according to a *Gallup Poll*.

Fear	*Individual Ranking*	*Team Ranking*
A. confined spaces	_____	_____
B. dogs	_____	_____
C. flying on a plane	_____	_____
D. heights	_____	_____
E. mice	_____	_____
F. needles and getting shots	_____	_____
G. public speaking	_____	_____
H. snakes	_____	_____
I. spiders and insects	_____	_____
J. thunder and lightning	_____	_____

Most Common Words

Of the thousands of words in the English language, these 10 words are the most common. Your task is to order the words from most common (number 1) to least common (number 10) based on the combined results of British English, American English, and Australian English surveys of contemporary sources in English: newspapers, magazines, books, TV, radio, and real life conversations— the language as it is written and spoken today.

Common Word	Individual Ranking	Team Ranking
A. a	_____	_____
B. and	_____	_____
C. in	_____	_____
D. is	_____	_____
E. it	_____	_____
F. of	_____	_____
G. that	_____	_____
H. the	_____	_____
I. to	_____	_____
J. you	_____	_____

Building Blocks

OBJECTIVES
- To understand the challenge of everyday communication
- To experience the role perception plays in our communication
- To experience the limitations of one-way communication

Group Size

  6 to 12

Materials

  Two identical sets of 15 interlocking
  Lego or Duplo blocks, paper, pens

Time

  30 to 40 minutes

Procedure

To keep everyone engaged, this activity works best for groups of up to 12, split into smaller teams of three to six. You can, however, use this activity with larger groups if you have plenty of space and blocks.

Split the group into two teams, Team A and Team B. Team A begins by building a structure out of blocks. While this is being done, take Team B to a location where they cannot see or hear Team A. As Team A is building the structure, they must write instructions on how to build their structure, because once it's completed, the challenge for Team B will be to rebuild Team A's structure based on the written instructions alone. After completion of the original structure, Team A takes the written instructions along with the blocks necessary to build an identical structure to Team B. After Team B has completed their structure, have someone from Team A bring the original structure to Team B for comparison.

Mid-Activity Discussion Questions

1. How accurate is Team B's structure?
2. How helpful were the written instructions?
3. What worked? What didn't?

Now it is Team B's turn. The process is repeated with Team B as the builders and instruction-writers and Team A as the rebuilders. The structures are compared again to see if the teams were able to improve the second time after lessons learned during the first round.

Tips

Depending on the group, you may choose to stipulate that a certain number of blocks be used (require they use all 15 blocks, for example). You may also want to mention that simply stacking one block on top of another is not permitted. The structure has to be able to stand on its own without toppling over.

Discussion Questions

1. How well did the other team follow your instructions?

2. How difficult was it to see the other team struggle with your instructions?

3. Can you give examples of other situations similar to this one?

4. How did your team's perception differ from the other team's perception?

5. What did you change during round two?

6. In what ways did this increase the understanding?

7. What did you learn?

Cross Over

Group Size

Any

Materials

20-foot rope tied in a knot, hula hoop, stopwatch

Time

30 to 40 minutes

Procedure

Place the rope on the ground in a circle and put the hoop on the ground in the middle of the rope. Have the team stand around the rope, bend down, and pick it up. Make sure the team is evenly spaced around the rope.

The objective is for team members to switch places with the people across from them in the circle, stepping one foot in the hoop as they cross the circle. There are two rules they must follow as they accomplish their objective: the rope cannot touch the ground and the hoop cannot be moved. Other than that, the team can do whatever it takes to meet the challenge of discovering as many solutions as they can while still following the rules.

Once the team is in position, give them their goal and challenge.

Goal: The team needs to see how fast everyone on the team can cross the circle stepping one foot in the hoop without dropping the rope.

Challenge: The team needs to find at least four solutions to the problem while adhering to the rules.

Rules: The rope cannot touch the ground. The hoop cannot be moved.

For each solution, have the team make a timed attempt.

Tips

- This is a great activity for early in your program as it gets participants to consider different perspectives, to listen, and to be open to others' ideas. Because these skills contribute to conflict resolution, it benefits a team to see the results of these skills early so they can use and build upon them.
- There are three activities to assist teams in multi-solution thinking: Cross Over, Hoop-la, and Speed Pass. The instructions are written for these three games in such a way as to stimulate creative interpretation. When pressed for rules for these games, simply state the basic rules and encourage teams to use their best judgment and turn to each other for answers.

Discussion Questions

1. What skills or characteristics did you have to use to discover additional solutions?
2. Were all ideas heard? Why or why not?
3. Do you usually take the time to discover additional solutions in conflict situations? Why not?
4. How difficult was it to come up with a fourth solution? Did you have to alter your thinking?
5. Which solution produced the best result? Why?
6. How would a conflict benefit from this technique?
7. What would you have to do that you usually don't do in those types of situations?
8. What kind of resolutions would you come to?
9. What is the likelihood the resolution would be a win-win resolution?

Hoop-La

OBJECTIVES

- To consider multiple solutions for solving a problem
- To collaborate as a team to solve problems

Group Size

8 to 12

Materials

Hula hoop (or 12-foot rope tied in a loop) and a stopwatch

Time

30 to 40 minutes

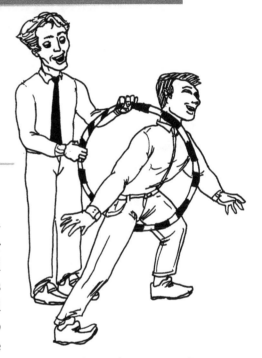

Procedure

Have the team join hands and form a circle. Ask two team members to break their connection so a hula hoop can be placed on their wrists between them. Once this is done, have them hold hands again. Tell the team that their task is to pass the hoop all the way around the circle, making sure that they maintain their connections (keep holding hands). Everyone's body has to pass through the hoop as it makes its way around the circle. The hoop finishes in the same place it started. After the practice round, ask for questions.

Now let them know you want to establish a base time for the task. Give them a "go" and let them begin, timing them this round. The clock starts on your "go" and ends when the hoop is back where it started. Once they have their base time, give them their challenge:

Goal: The team needs to see how fast they can move the hoop around the circle.

Challenge: The team needs to find at least four solutions to the problem.

Rules: The team has to maintain their connection at all times (hold hands). Everyone's body has to pass through the hoop. The hoop starts on the wrists of two team members and ends where it started. No outside help is allowed (the team cannot use props to secure the hoop or have the facilitator or observers hold the hoop).

For each solution, have the team make a timed attempt.

Hint: The team does not have to remain in a "circle"; they simply have to have a closed loop of people, but it is better to let them figure this out on their own.

Tips
- This is a great activity for early in your program as it gets participants to consider different perspectives, to listen, and to be open to others' ideas. Because these skills contribute to conflict resolution, it benefits a team to see the results of these skills early so they can use and build upon them.
- There are three activities to assist teams in multi-solution thinking: Cross Over, Hoop-La, and Speed Pass. The instructions are written for these three games in such a way as to stimulate creative interpretation. When pressed for rules for these games, simply state the basic rules and encourage teams to use their best judgment and turn to each other for answers.

Discussion Questions
1. What skills or characteristics did you use to discover additional solutions?
2. Were all ideas heard? Why or why not?
3. Do you usually take the time to discover additional solutions in conflict situations? Why or why not?
4. Which solution resulted in the best time?
5. What might this tell us about the benefits of looking for the "second" or "third" right answer?
6. How would a conflict benefit from this technique?
7. What would you need to do that you usually don't do in those types of situations?
8. What kind of resolution would you come to?
9. What is the likelihood the resolution would be a win-win resolution?

Speed Pass

Group Size

8 to 12

Materials

Tennis ball and stopwatch

Time

30 to 40 minutes

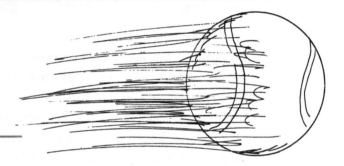

Procedure

Start with your team in a circle. Begin tossing the tennis ball around, establishing a pattern. Each player gets the ball only once. It starts and ends with the facilitator. Once the pattern is established, the facilitator steps out of the circle to become the official timekeeper. The person the facilitator originally threw the ball to starts and finishes the sequence. Give the team one practice round to make sure the adjustment is made.

Now the team is ready to play. Ask the team to toss the ball through the sequence while you time them to get a base time. The ball starts and ends with the same person. Make sure they know what the base time is. Next, give them their goal and challenge.

Goal: The team needs to see how fast they can move the ball through the sequence.

Challenge: The team needs to find at least four solutions to the problem.

Rules: The ball has to follow the established pattern and each player must have sole possession for a brief moment in time (this eliminates one person taking control of the ball and simply swiping it across everyone's hands).

For each solution, have the team make a timed attempt. Examples of solutions a team may find: standing in the original circle and passing the ball as fast as they can; switching places so they are standing next to the person they pass to; keeping the ball stationary while everyone touches it in order; or rolling the ball down everyone's hands.

Hint: The team does not have to remain in a circle, although it's best to let them figure this out on their own.

Tips

- This is a great activity for early in your program as it gets participants to consider different perspectives, to listen, and to be open to others' ideas. Because these skills contribute to conflict resolution, it benefits a team to see the results of these skills early so they can use and build upon them.
- There are three activities to assist teams in multi-solution thinking: Cross Over, Hoop-La, and Speed Pass. The instructions are written for these three games in such a way as to stimulate creative interpretation. When pressed for rules for these games, simply state the basic rules and encourage teams to use their best judgment and turn to each other for answers.

Variations

Some variations of this activity recommend using a koosh ball. For this challenge, a tennis ball works the best and contributes to more solutions.

Discussion Questions

1. What skills or characteristics did you use to discover additional solutions?
2. Were all ideas heard? Why or why not?
3. Do you usually take the time to discover additional solutions in conflict situations? Why or why not?
4. Of your solutions, which one gave you the best time? What can we learn from that?
5. How would a conflict benefit from this multi-solution technique?
6. What would you have to do that you usually don't do in those types of situations?
7. What kind of resolution would you come to?
8. What is the likelihood the resolution would be a win-win resolution?

6

EQ (Emotional Intelligence)

Any fool can know. The point is to understand.

—Albert Einstein

Behind the Mask

Group Size

Any

Materials

One copy of Behind the Mask Questions handout (provided) for the facilitator; one copy of My Mask handout (provided) and a pen for each participant

Time

20 to 30 minutes

Procedure

Give everyone a My Mask handout. Ask them to use their pens to punch some holes in the mask where the eyes and mouth are. Invite them to flip the mask handout over because they will be using the back side to write their answers to 20 questions (handout provided). They can write anywhere on the back of the page.

After they finish answering the questions, have them turn their handout over so the mask is showing and begin the debrief discussion.

Tips

For the debriefing, if your group is large, form teams of four to seven participants and hand out a copy of the discussion questions to each team for a table discussion before the large group discussion.

Discussion Questions

1. If you hold the masks up to your face and look around at your teammates, do you see any of the elements and characteristics that make each of us who we are?

2. Even though the qualities and characteristics are not apparent at first glance, do they impact our interactions with others? In what ways?

3. While we are not going to ask anyone to divulge the answers to the 20 questions, what are the chances that your answers match with anyone else's?

4. In what ways does diversity contribute to a more effective team?

5. How do our unique qualities relate to perspective?

6. How is this helpful in a conflict?

7. How would it influence the outcome if we were to switch masks with the person with whom we are in conflict?

8. What are some things we could do when in conflict with another person that would have a similar effect as switching masks?

Behind the Mask Questions

1. What is your gender?

2. How old are you?

3. How many siblings do you have?

4. What is your position in the family (oldest, only, youngest, middle)?

5. Are you married or single?

6. How many children do you have?

7. Where did you grow up?

8. What is your ethnic background?

9. What languages do you speak?

10. What is your job title?

11. How long have you been at your job?

12. What is your favorite music?

13. What activities do you enjoy in your leisure time?

14. Write down three people who have influenced you in your life. How have they influenced you? Be specific.

15. Are you a talker or a listener?

16. Do you form quick judgments or do you ask questions?

17. Do you see problems or opportunities?

18. Are you emotional or logical?

19. Are you patient or impatient?

20. What are your "words to live by"?

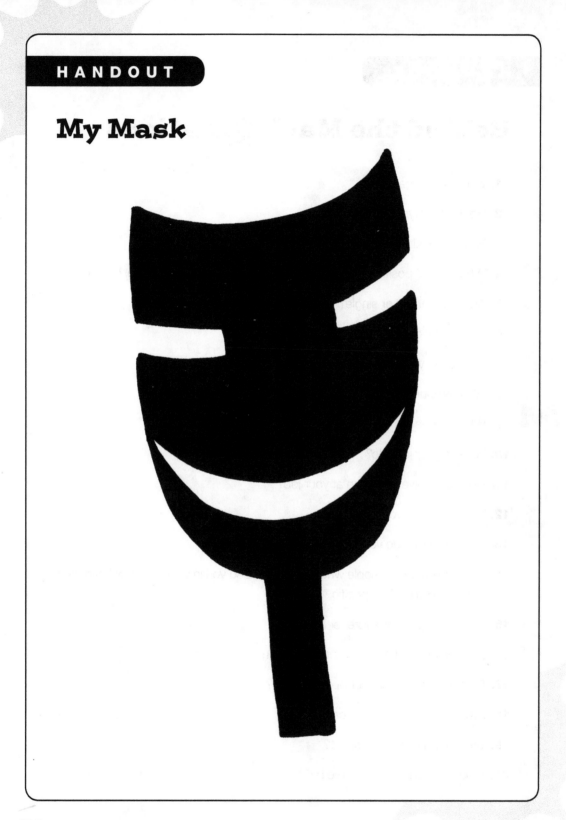

My Mask

Shoes

Group Size
Any

Materials
Two cutouts of the Shoe Template handout (provided) for each person and markers

Time
15 to 20 minutes

Procedure

This can be either a powerful EQ activity or a lighter perspective activity. At the start of the program, after the introduction and icebreakers, give each team member two Shoe Template handouts. Allow a few minutes for them to customize their shoes, so they can identify their shoes throughout the day.

Our first reaction to any situation is an emotional reaction. In times of conflict, the emotional reaction can take over and control the process. Explain that our emotional intelligence (EQ) is our ability to understand our and others' emotions and be aware of those emotions as they happen. The goal is to use that awareness to effectively manage our interactions with others. During times of conflict, EQ is a valuable skill that can lead to a collaborative outcome. This activity will allow team members to check out their perceptions and to improve their EQ.

If, at some time during the training, team members feel they are not being heard or understood, they can present their shoe to another person, at which time the person to whom the shoe is presented communicates the situation from the shoe-giver's perspective.

It becomes a more powerful EQ activity with an end-of-session debriefing discussion, which provides time for reflection and consideration.

Variations

Rather than giving out the template shoes, provide paper, scissors, and pens and have participants create their own shoes. This version is a fun, creative way to begin the day.

Discussion Questions

1. Does anyone still have one or both of their shoes left?
2. Do we usually take the time to make sure we understand each other's perspective?
3. For those of you who received a shoe, what can we all learn from that?
4. For those of you who gave both shoes away, what can the team learn from that?
5. What are some reasons we don't take the time to make sure we understand each other's perspectives? How does this impact the team?
6. How does it benefit us as individuals and the team overall to respect everyone's perspective?
7. What can we do to make sure everyone's perspective is understood?
8. Do we all communicate in the same manner?
9. How can we accommodate each other's communication styles?

Shoe Template

Let's Face It

Group Size
Any

Materials
Slips of paper, pens

Time
10 to 20 minutes

Procedure

Facial expressions are an important part of communication. While there are many emotions and corresponding facial expressions, some are easier to interpret than others. This activity allows team members to experience the effect of different expressions and how facial expressions impact communication and understanding.

Split large groups into teams of four to 10 people. With large groups that are split into smaller teams, have each team select a team facilitator for the activity. (A quick and easy way to do this is to have everyone on the team point their index fingers to the ceiling, and on the count of three drop their arms and point to the person they would like to appoint as their facilitator.) The team facilitator's job is to keep the activity moving and to lead the debriefing discussion for the team.

Each team member writes one emotion on a small slip of paper, then folds the slip of paper and gives it to the team facilitator. Now the team members, in turn, each take one of the folded slips and do their best to convey the emotion to the rest of the team (using facial expressions only). The other members of the team do their best to interpret the facial expression and emotion being enacted.

Tips
Have team members contribute two or three emotions for a longer activity. Print out the discussion questions so each team has a copy.

Discussion Questions
1. How significant are facial expressions in conveying our emotions?
2. What are some situations in which facial expressions are crucial in communication and comprehension?
3. What emotions are the easiest to comprehend? Why?
4. What emotions are not easy to interpret? Why?
5. What facial expressions are easiest to misinterpret?
6. What effect do facial expressions have on our interactions with others?
7. How aware are we of our facial expressions?
8. How do facial expressions consciously or unconsciously impact our ability to resolve conflict?
9. Given what we learned here, is it possible to better manage our nonverbal communication? How?

Knot It

Group Size

Any

Materials

Five ropes (between 6 and 10 feet in length) for each team and Knot It Observer
Form handout (provided)

Time

30 to 40 minutes

Procedure

Split the group into teams of six. Team members need to arrange themselves in one long line, holding a rope between each of them. The people at the end will be holding only one rope. Once they are in position, explain that they cannot let go of their rope for the duration of the activity. The team's challenge is to tie a knot in the center rope. Because this game is deceptively difficult, you may want to recommend that the team imagine themselves as one long rope—the team members are just extensions of that rope. Once they understand the goal, have them begin. If anyone loses contact with the rope, the team has to start over.

Observers can provide valuable perspective during the debriefing discussion for this activity. For anyone uncomfortable with the activity level, or if you have more people than required for the game, give them the Knot It Observer Form (provided) to focus their attention and keep them engaged throughout the process.

Variations
The facilitator pre-ties one knot in each rope used for the game. Players arrange themselves by holding a rope between them, just like the original game. But unlike the original game, the goal for the group is to untie the knots as quickly as possible without letting go of the rope.

Discussion Questions
1. What did you notice during the challenge?
2. Was the activity more difficult than you anticipated?
3. How did the team react to the surprising difficulty of reaching your goal?
4. How did you express your frustration?
5. Did you notice the frustration level of anyone else on the team? Can you give examples?
6. In what ways did you and the team address emotions?
7. Do we face similar communication challenges at work?
8. What are some ways in which inaccurate assumptions lead to conflict?
9. What steps can we take to prevent this from occurring?

Knot It Observer Form

During the activity, please take a moment to answer these questions.

1. Did the teams initially see this challenge as easy?

_____

2. How did the team members react to the difficulty of reaching the goal?

_____

3. Did the difficulty level result in conflict? If so, how was the conflict resolved?

_____

4. How effective was the communication during the activity? Give examples.

_____

5. What did the team do well?

_____

6. Additional comments:

_____

_____

Hot Buttons

Group Size

Any

Materials

Paper, pens

Time

15 to 20 minutes

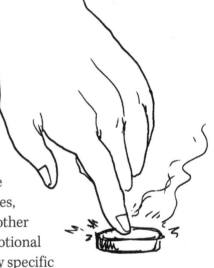

Procedure

Tell the participants that it's time to release some pent-up stress. For the next five minutes, they are going to get a chance to tell the other members of their team how to push their emotional hot buttons. Ask them to write down as many specific things as they can. For example:

How to push my buttons . . .

- Rude tone
- "Shut up!"
- Bad grammar
- Pushy individuals
- Whining
- Know-it-alls
- "What you should do is . . ."
- People who don't get to the point
- "You never/always . . ."

Tips

Have teams of four to seven see how many emotional hot buttons they can come up with.

Discussion Questions

1. Now that you are aware of some of your emotional hot buttons, what can you do about it?

2. What are some ways we can learn to recognize and to control our hot buttons when interacting with others?

3. What if we push someone else's buttons?

4. How does this activity help us deal with conflict more effectively?

Get the Memo

Group Size
Up to 10

Materials
Slips of paper, pens

Time
15 to 20 minutes

MEMO

TO:
FROM:
DATE:
RE:

Procedure

Give each person a slip of paper and a pen. Let them know they will be writing a short memo to someone on the team. Instruct them to write three things on their paper:

To: Have them write the name of any other person on the team here.
From: Have them write their own name here.
Task: Have them write a task that they would like the person in the "To" line to perform in front of the team (for example, do three jumping jacks, say the alphabet backward).

After they have completed their memos, have them fold them in half so the information is confidential. Collect all the memos. Ask the team to form a circle and tell them that as you read the assigned tasks, they are to quickly go into the center of the circle and carry out the task. Read the first memo and instruct the person in the "From" line to perform the task he or she has given to the person in the "To" line. Quickly go through all the memos and have each person perform the task originally intended for his or her "To" person. Don't be surprised if you hear a few groans as they begin to understand that they have to do what they wanted someone else to do.

Tips

You can make this work for larger groups by splitting them into teams of up to 10 and appointing someone from the team to the role of facilitator.

Discussion Questions

1. What was your first reaction when you realized you would have to perform your own tasks?
2. Do we ever expect others to do things that we ourselves are unwilling to do?
3. If this is the case, how does having a diverse team work to our benefit?
4. For this activity, we literally had to put ourselves in someone else's intended shoes. How did that feel?
5. Do we always take the time to consider other perspectives? Why not?
6. How might this affect the conflict-resolution process?

The Shoe's on the Other Foot

Group Size

Any

Materials

One copy of The Shoe's on the Other Foot handout (provided) for each person, pens

Time

5 to 10 minutes

Procedure

Pass out the handout to each participant and have them take five minutes to complete their handout on an individual basis, followed by a small-group discussion.

Tips

This handout can provide valuable insight as part of a mid-activity discussion during an activity that is producing a high level of frustration or conflict.

Discussion Questions

1. We can improve our EQ by becoming more aware of other people's emotions and how they play a factor in our interactions. How did it feel to be in another person's shoes?

2. In what ways did your understanding of the other person's perspective change?

3. What are some ways we can make sure we are interpreting someone else's emotions accurately in a nonconfrontational manner?

4. In what ways might this influence the likelihood of transforming conflict into something productive?

5. How does this activity benefit the team?

6. What will you do differently the next time you're involved in a conflict?

The Shoe's on the Other Foot

Think back to a situation where you were in conflict with another person. Carefully consider the other person's perspective while answering these questions. Remember to look at the situation *only* from the *other* person's viewpoint.

1. In your opinion, what is/was the issue?

_____

_____

_____

3. What caused it?

_____

_____

_____

4. What are you feeling?

_____

_____

_____

5. How would you describe the event?

_____

_____

_____

6. What would you like to have happen to resolve the conflict?

_____

_____

_____

Tied Up in Knots

Group Size

10 to 25

Materials

50-foot rope, tape

Time

15 to 30 minutes

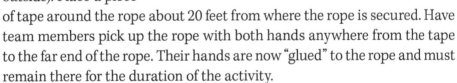

Procedure

Secure one end of the rope to a stationary object such as a door-knob (or a light pole or telephone pole, if outside). Place a piece of tape around the rope about 20 feet from where the rope is secured. Have team members pick up the rope with both hands anywhere from the tape to the far end of the rope. Their hands are now "glued" to the rope and must remain there for the duration of the activity.

The team must now tie a knot in the rope so it falls between where the rope is secured and the piece of tape.

Tips

Usually it takes two or three attempts. On the rare occasion, teams get this the first time out—if this happens, have the team do it again, saying that you are looking for a standardized knot-tying process. Because they figured it out so fast, it should be no problem to do it again. This, however, is not usually the case, which the team learns very quickly. Sometimes this second attempt leads to even more frustration and communication problems than if they didn't get it so fast the first time around.

Discussion Questions

1. What did you notice during the activity?
2. In what ways did emotions surface? Why did you feel the way you did?
3. Were you aware of other team members' emotions? How were you made aware?
4. Are emotions obstacles to goal achievement or part of the process?
5. Are emotions good or bad?
6. During times of conflict, how does it benefit us or the team to be more aware of our and others' emotions?
7. What did you do to achieve success?
8. Were all ideas heard? Why or why not?
9. Did your plan change along the way?
10. How did the communication change throughout the process?

7

Collaboration

Alone we can do so little; together we can do so much.

—Helen Keller

Personality Plus

Group Size

Any

Materials

One copy of the Personality Plus handout (provided) for each person, pens

Time

15 to 20 minutes

Procedure

Collaboration is defined as the act of working together to achieve a goal. In teams, collaboration drives creativity because new and better things always emerge from a series of ideas rather than a single insight. With this activity, we will explore the team's tendencies toward collaboration.

First, pass out the Personality Plus handout to each team member. Give them a few minutes to work on the questions individually, and then allow them to work in teams of four to seven. After 15 minutes, go over their answers and the discussion questions. At the conclusion of the group discussion, have individuals share their answers to question number 7 on the handout either with their team or with the whole group.

Variations

Instead of collaboration, use diversity as the skill of the team.

Discussion Questions

The handout questions can serve as the debriefing questions, but here are some additional questions:

1. As a team, did you generally agree on our team's personality? Why or why not?

2. How did it help you to hear other team members' perspective of our team?

3. As a team, what are some ways we can improve our personality to promote more collaboration?

Personality Plus

1. If our team was a person, how would you describe its personality traits?

_____

_____

_____

2. Does its personality support collaboration?

_____

_____

_____

3. What traits specifically support collaboration?

_____

_____

_____

4. What traits specifically impede collaboration?

_____

_____

_____

5. What are some additional traits we could work on to improve our ability to collaborate?

_____

_____

_____

6. What can we do individually to enhance the personality of our team?

_____

_____

_____

7. What will you commit to doing to enhance the personality of our team?

_____

_____

_____

It's a What?

OBJECTIVES
- To understand obstacles to collaboration
- To experience the collaborative process

Group Size
   Any
Materials
   Paper, markers
Time
   10 to 15 minutes

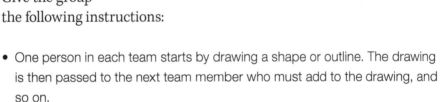

Procedure
Split the group into teams of three to five participants. Give the group the following instructions:

- One person in each team starts by drawing a shape or outline. The drawing is then passed to the next team member who must add to the drawing, and so on.
- Time spent by each person in turn on the drawing is limited to five seconds. (The facilitator can shout "change" when the time is up.)
- No discussion is permitted during the drawing, nor any agreement before the drawing of what the team will draw.
- The drawing must be completed in one minute.

Discussion Questions

1. Did your team draw anything recognizable?
2. How easy was the understanding between team members?
3. How did team members work differently on this task?
4. What was the effect of time pressure?
5. Was there a natural tendency to draw supportively and harmoniously, or were there more conflicting ideas?
6. What was your expectation of the completed drawing?
7. Did your expectation change? Why?
8. Why was it important to maintain an open mind?
9. How does flexibility relate to collaboration?
10. What pressure did the time element have on your experience?
11. How does stress and pressure affect our willingness to collaborate?
12. Why may it be important to collaborate during times of stress and pressure?

Creative Collaboration

OBJECTIVES
- To experience the creative process collaboratively
- To tap into the creativity of the team

Group Size

Any

Materials

Slips of paper, pens, paper bag

Time

15 to 20 minutes

Procedure

This game is played in two rounds. Break large groups into smaller teams of four to seven. While teams don't have to have the exact same number of participants, it should be close.

This activity uses the creative thinking technique called "concept combination." This involves taking two concepts or objects and combining them in some novel way. For example, what can you come up with from the combination of a baseball hat and a rock, or an iPod and a cooler, or a hair dryer and a bike?

Have each participant write down the name of an object on a slip of paper and place it in a paper bag. After collecting all the slips, have someone randomly pick two slips of paper from the bag to be used by all teams in the first round of the activity. Read the items aloud and invite the teams to brainstorm to come up with a way to combine these two objects in a creative and innovative manner. Teams have six minutes to come up with the best idea. After the time is up, have each team present their idea to the group.

In the second round, have someone from each team randomly pick two slips of paper from the bag. The team now must brainstorm to come up with a way to combine their two new and different objects in a creative and innovative manner.

After six minutes, have each team present their best idea to the group.

Discussion Questions

1. What was challenging about this activity?

2. What did you notice regarding the team brainstorming?

3. What were some differences in the two rounds?

4. Was the manner in which you brainstormed the same for both rounds? Why or why not?

5. How does the assumption of competition impact our ability to collaborate?

6. During the first round, did you or your team try to prevent other teams from hearing your ideas? What about the second round? How did this affect your ability to brainstorm?

7. In the first round, did you hear any other team's comments that led your team to more creative ideas?

8. What is challenging about collaboration?

9. What are the benefits of collaboration?

10. What are some real-life situations that benefit from collaboration?

Stump the Facilitator

Group Size

12 to 20

Materials

None

Time

20 to 30 minutes

Procedure

Tell the team that they are going to have a chance to play the exciting game of Stump the Facilitator. Have the team sit in a circle. During the game, they will be performing different activities like clapping, snapping fingers, stomping feet, and so on. Each different movement has to be initiated by one person in the group. Once everyone catches on, someone else can take the lead and initiate a different movement (everyone has to be demonstrating an action before it can be changed). The team adopts the new action, and then a third movement is initiated by a different leader. The team's goal is to make it impossible for the facilitator to determine who the initiator is by making the transitions as discreet as possible.

The whole time this is going on, the facilitator is searching the circle to see if he or she can catch the team making the switch and name the person who initiated the action. For example, if Jack starts to clap, everyone else should clap. Once everyone is clapping, Katie could discreetly start to snap her fingers; after everyone makes the switch to snapping fingers, Russell might begin stomping his foot, and so on. The only rule is that a team member can only perform one movement at a time (Russell can't snap and stomp simultaneously).

Let them know you will leave the room for two minutes to allow them time to strategize. It will probably take a few rounds before they coordinate their actions and make a collaborative effort to work together seamlessly. Once they get proficient, you could give them a time goal, such as, "See if you can go for three minutes before I guess who the initiator is." Another option at this point would be to ask if a team member would like to volunteer to be "stumped."

Tips
The larger the group, the harder it is to figure out who the initiator is.

Discussion Questions
1. Did you compete over who was the leader? If so, what happened as a result?
2. What strategy was effective?
3. How did you communicate during the game?
4. What are some ways in which communication challenges lead to conflict?
5. How can we communicate to promote collaboration?
6. When teams collaborate, there is a flow to it—did you experience flow in this activity? Have you ever experienced flow at work? What does it take to get to that stage of collaboration?

Build a Word

Group Size

At least 8

Materials

26 index cards for each team, markers, paper, rubber bands

Time

20 to 30 minutes

Procedure

Divide the group into teams of four to eight. Give each team 26 index cards, some markers, one blank piece of paper, and a rubber band.

Ask the teams to put aside one index card and write one letter on each of the remaining 25 index cards. Let them know that they will be using the index cards to build as many words as possible. Each card can be used only one time in each word, so teams may choose multiples of common letters. Give teams five minutes to collectively decide which letters to write on their cards. After the team has completed their cards, ask them to put them in a stack and rubber-band them together.

The next step is to have each team set a goal for the number of words they will be able to generate using their stack of cards. Have them write this number on the remaining index card and place it with the stack.

Now for the twist—each team trades their stack of cards with another team, keeping the cards stacked facedown in the middle of their table or area. Once everyone has a new stack of cards, let them know that they have seven minutes to come up with as many different words as possible using the new stack of cards (keeping the goal in mind). Have teams assign one person as their scribe who will write the words the team creates on the blank piece of paper. Give them the go-ahead to begin.

When the time is up, have teams report their total words to the group.

Tips
Take note of how the addition of the goal impacts the process, the stress level, and the communication within teams and the group as a whole.

Discussion Questions
1. How did you choose what letters to write?
2. What was your initial plan as you chose your letters?
3. What, if anything, would you have done differently had you known about the "twist" as you were choosing letters?
4. How did you figure out the goal?
5. How did you feel when you had to reach the goal set by another team?
6. What adjustments did your team make?
7. Was time lost regrouping or readjusting? Why?
8. Did anyone ask for help from the team of origin? Why or why not?
9. In what ways do we benefit from challenges such as this?
10. What situations can we equate this experience to?
11. What can we learn from this activity?

Super Stars

Group Size

6 to 16

Materials

Painter's tape, Super Stars Grid handout (provided); 16 star-shaped markers (six of one color, six of a second color, and four of a third color; you can use 5-inch foam stars found at craft stores or make your own out of construction paper; one copy of the Super Stars Rules handout (provided) for each team; one copy of the Super Stars Score Sheet handout (provided) for the facilitator; a Super Stars Observer Form handout (provided) for each observer; pens

Time

40 to 60 minutes

Procedure

Using the painter's tape, create a 4-foot by 4-foot grid on the floor (see Super Stars Grid for an example).

Split your team into two groups of three to eight (groups do not have to have the exact same number of people). If you have more than eight people for each small group, any additional group members can act as observers (up to three observers are plenty). Give each group six stars of one color and two additional "wild" stars. Wild stars are the same color for both groups. For example, give one group six blue stars and two yellow wild stars; give the other group six green stars and two yellow wild stars.

Provide a Super Stars Rules handout for each group and an Observer Form for any observers.

This game is played in a series of rounds (typically three to five). At the end of each round, the facilitator tallies the points and records them on the score sheet so everyone can see the results. If, after posting the scores, someone asks if both sides can work together, you can reiterate, "Your goal is to get the maximum number of points possible." If they continue to pressure you, request that they refer to their rules sheet for guidance.

When I facilitate this activity, I don't say I am adding all the points together, I just do it. In fact, I usually post the scores after the first round is over and as they are planning their strategy for the second round. Scores usually don't amount to much in the first round because both sides are so focused on preventing the other side from scoring; they use all their resources to block rather than score. After the first round, the lightbulbs should start to go off as some observant group members begin to realize that they need to cooperate rather than compete with each other. It is interesting to see if their group agrees or continues to compete.

Make sure to enforce the rule about not talking to the other group. Once they begin to work together and share resources, give them one last round to see how high a score they can generate by working together.

Eventually it should become clear that for the team to be successful both groups need to be successful and cooperative. Blocking the other group only serves to waste resources and results in a low score for both groups and the team overall. Even though the rules specifically state, "Your goal is to accumulate the maximum number of points possible," few groups consider a win-win option and instead immediately compete with the other group. It is interesting to note that when the groups begin to trust and collaborate, the rounds are faster and more fun. Pay attention to how the energy shifts during the activity as well, or ask the observers to notice the difference in the energy as the groups begin to work together.

Tips

If the groups are not moving in the direction of cooperation by the third round, you may consider requiring them to play a wild star by the third placement, and another one by the sixth placement.

It's a good idea to practice this game with some friends or family first. Many groups will figure it out in three rounds, but for some it takes more. If groups get locked into the competition mode, set a time limit for placing their stars; otherwise, this game can take far too long and some will lose interest and get frustrated (if this happens, use it in the debriefing discussion).

Discussion Questions

1. What were some of your initial thoughts regarding this game?
2. What plan took shape?
3. Did your plan change along the way?
4. How was trust a factor?
5. What did you think or do when the other group did not respond the way you thought they would?
6. As you began to share your resources and work together, how did the energy change?
7. What did you notice as you started to collaborate rather than compete?
8. How does this activity relate to the workplace and working with other departments?

Super Stars Grid

This layout produces the highest score. Here, each group would score 100 points, for a team total of 200 points.

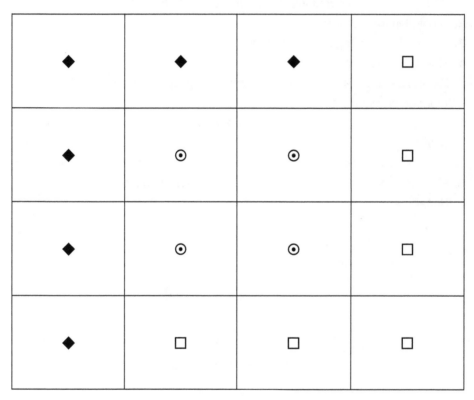

Group A ☐   Group B ◆   Wild ⊙

Super Stars Rules

1. No talking to the other group at any time during the game.

2. Your goal is to accumulate the maximum number of points possible.

3. There are 10 points scored for three stars in a row. Rows can be vertical, horizontal, or diagonal.

4. Groups take turns placing their stars on the grid until all stars have been placed.

5. A different group starts each round of play.

6. Wild stars can be played any time and may be counted by either group.

7. Once a star has been played, it can't be moved.

8. Groups have three minutes to plan between rounds of play.

Super Stars Score Sheet

Round	Blue Stars	Green Stars	Team
1.			
2.			
3.			
4.			
5.			

Super Stars Observer Form

During the activity, please take a moment to answer these questions.

1. Did the teams see this as a competition? Explain.

_____

2. How did the teams demonstrate trust? Provide examples.

_____

3. How easily did the two groups embrace the idea of collaboration?

_____

4. What resistance did you notice?

_____

5. How did the energy change when the two groups began to work as one team?

_____

6. Additional comments:

_____

_____

_____

Quotable Quotes

Group Size
Any
Materials
Cardstock, markers
Time
15 to 20 minutes

Procedure

Break your group into six teams (teams of four to seven work best). With groups larger than 42, divide them in such a way as to have 12 teams, with two teams getting each concept.

Each team is given one step of the six steps of conflict resolution (listed below). Each group creates a quotation, slogan, or "words to live by" regarding their step of the process. After 10 minutes, have the teams share their quotations with the entire group. Put the quotations on the wall for the duration of the program.

Steps to Conflict Resolution

1. Acknowledge the conflict.
2. Identify the real conflict.
3. Listen to all points of view.
4. Together, look for ways to resolve the conflict.
5. Get agreement on a resolution.
6. Follow up to review the resolution.

Tips

During subsequent debriefing discussions, refer to their quotations whenever applicable to create buy-in and ownership.

Variations

Use this activity following Step by Step, where the team identifies the steps to conflict resolution. Make sure you have the same number of teams as steps in the process.

Discussion Questions

1. In what ways do these slogans or "words to live by" help us become more comfortable with conflict?

2. How does becoming more comfortable with the idea of conflict help us to become better at dealing with the conflicts in our lives?

Monumental

OBJECTIVES
- To create collaboratively
- To review and recap the concept of conflict resolution

Group Size
Any
Materials
Random items provided by participants; a camera
is optional
Time
15 to 20 minutes

Procedure

During a break, ask everyone to bring back
one or two random items (rock, a stapler, a
plant). Make sure to tell them they will be
able to retrieve their items at the end of the
session.

At the conclusion of a conflict-resolution
program, split any large groups into teams
of about seven or eight participants. Tell
team members they are to create a monu-
ment to the concept of conflict resolution, which they will be presenting
to the group. Each part of the monument needs to represent something
specific they learned about the concept. Each person must contribute at
least one random item, and it's up to the team to creatively make it fit
with the theme of the monument. Allow 10 to 15 minutes and begin the
presentations.

Tips

Take a picture of each team with their monument as a takeaway and a
great memory trigger.

Discussion Questions

1. In what ways did you collaborate to build your monuments?

2. What was challenging? What was fun?

3. What will you remember?

About the Author

Mary Scannell, founder of BizTeamTools.com, puts theory into practice by leading nearly 100 corporate trainings per year, throughout the United States and Canada. She has trained tens of thousands of students and businesspeople, including a long list of Fortune 500 clients.

Mary's expertise in games and group activities extends through the full gamut of the topic—from small classroom exercises to large-scale outdoor adventure events.

CPSIA information can be obtained
at www.ICGtesting.com
Printed in the USA
BVHW091309081222
653655BV00003B/3

9 780071 836715